DATE DUE

APR 9 1986	JUN 3 1994
MAY 9 1986	JUN 0 8 REC'D NOV 0 4 1997
MAY 2 0 1986	
OCT 2 2 1986	NOV 2 4 1997
FEB 2 0 1987	NOV 1 7 1997
NOV 5 1987	
NOV 1 1 1987	
FEB 1 5 1988	
JAN 2 7 1988	
AUG 2 6 1988	
NOV 8 1988	
MAY 1 0 1989	
OCT 2 7 1989	
OCT 2 4 1989	
APR 1 8 1991	
APR 1 7 1991	

The Love That Never Faileth

Barbara B. Smith

Bookcraft
Salt Lake City, Utah

Library of Congress Catalog Card Number: 84-71989
ISBN 0-88494-542-1

2 3 4 5 6 7 8 9 10   89 88 87 86 85 84

Lithographed in the United States of America
PUBLISHERS PRESS
Salt Lake City, Utah

To my husband and family

for the renewing dedication of their love

Contents

Preface

Over the years of my administration as the general president of the Relief Society I have been privileged to travel widely and be with the women of the Church. Through the miracle of electronic development I have been allowed to speak to millions in interviews and broadcast talks. In the turmoil of public debates that erupted and continued most of that decade over the role of woman, ranging widely from her rights to her responsibilities, I have been drawn into considerable discussion over fundamental issues defining a woman's significance in the work of building the kingdom of God and the work of the world.

Over and over again as I have prepared and presented my ideas to thoughtful, attentive groups of women, and been engaged with them in thousands of conversations, I have found love to be the single most often recurring theme. Love is the force that binds the women of the Church together in a sisterhood that transcends all of our differences. It is the motivating force in our lives and the sustaining strength in our trials. Very early in my administration, I was made aware of the great love of the Lord for his daughters, and I soon came to appreciate the reality of love as the source of life and renewal which is eternal.

The love of which the Lord speaks is a nurturing power that makes it possible for us to do more things than we ever dreamed possible. It is love that the word of God seeks to kindle in our souls, that we might have light and be persuaded to serve one another.

It is no wonder that the organization given to the women of the Church is one whose purposes are based on charity, the pure love of Christ. We are directed to do the work we have seen him do. The woman's responsibility is love—to give it, to share it, to teach it, to receive it. Love is eternal. It is one thing that never faileth.

The love I have seen expressed leads onward to that perfection we seek to attain. The more nearly we understand and apply the many facets of love in our lives, the greater the comfort and peace we feel. In this compilation of thoughts drawn largely from talks given during my service as the tenth general president of the Relief Society are diverse expressions of that concept of never-failing love, for I found that great teaching to offer the most hope to women of all ages and in all circumstances.

I would like to express appreciation to the prophet of the Lord who extended this exciting, demanding, humbling call to me. It has been an unparalleled opportunity for which I am profoundly grateful.

I am grateful to a number of people who have given me help in the preparation of this manuscript.

—To Moana B. Bennett for her help in writing and editing.

—To Helen Pehrson, my secretary, for her tireless efforts in preparing the manuscript.

—And finally to my counselors, Marian R. Boyer, Janath R. Cannon, Shirley W. Thomas, and Ann S. Reese; to Mayola R. Miltenberger, general secretary-treasurer, and members of the Relief Society general board; and to the women of the Church for their support, for their receptive listening, and for inspiring me unendingly with the love and dedication of their own lives.

Prologue

On Commencing the Call

When you said, "Oh no!" as President Belle S. Spafford's name was presented for an honorable release just now, so did I. Many times when Relief Society conference was over I have sat here in the Tabernacle and thanked our Heavenly Father that Sister Spafford was still our general president.

When President Kimball came to my home and called me to be the general president of the Relief Society, I could not believe that it was happening to me. I controlled my emotions pretty well until he left. And then I wept and I wept and I wept.

I have dreaded this moment, for I knew what your reaction would be. As I heard that great sound of your hearts my tears began to flow again and I did not think I would have the courage to walk up here and stand at this podium, let alone speak to you regarding my acceptance of this call. As I waited to be invited to come forward, words from the song "How Firm A Foundation," filled my mind and calmed my troubled soul. "Fear not, I am with thee, O be not dismayed, / For I am thy God and will still give

Talk given on October 3, 1974, at the Relief Society general conference after being sustained as general president.

thee aid; / I'll strengthen thee, help thee, and cause thee to stand, / Upheld by my righteous, omnipotent hand." (*Hymns,* no. 66.) A peace filled me sufficiently to allow me to stand now and express some of my feelings.

I am humbly grateful for this calling and consider it a signal honor, and I am grateful for the privilege that has been mine to serve the past four years under the magnificent leadership of President Spafford. I love her. I love her counselors, Sister Marianne C. Sharp and Sister Louise W. Madsen, the general secretary-treasurer Sister Mayola R. Miltenberger, and every member of the Relief Society General Board. Working with them has been a great pleasure and I have enjoyed serving on this board.

I can see wisdom in releasing Sister Spafford and not letting her stay in this position until she passes away. She should be able to give of her vast reservoir of information regarding Relief Society to someone else.

I sat with her for many hours one Saturday afternoon while she told me of the many responsibilities she has shouldered as the general president. Then she asked, "Have I worn you out?" And I said, "No. You have merely confirmed what I knew to be true." I know this is a great work and carries with it heavy responsibilities.

But I love the Lord with all my heart and I desire to serve him well. I know that he lives, that he answers prayers, that he is concerned for each one of us; that he gives us the strength to be able to fulfill the callings he gives us. I will try to live worthy of this great trust. I am thankful for the faith in me of our beloved First Presidency. I honor and revere them. I know that President Kimball is the prophet of God upon the earth today.

I am grateful for these marvelous women who have accepted the calling to serve as my counselors. I know that you will love them and that you will come to appreciate their great worth. I am grateful beyond measure for a husband who loves me and will support me. I love my children. We have seven and I know that they, along with their good companions, will give me their total support. One son said, "When Mother is called to a responsibility she involves the whole family. We all should be set apart."

It is a wonderful thing to know that you can call upon your children and they will respond to each request. I know they will live worthy of this responsibility.

As I think about Sister Spafford today, I remember the words of Ruth to Naomi when she said, "Intreat me not to leave thee, or to return from following after thee: for whither thou goest, I will go; and where thou lodgest, I will lodge: thy people shall be my people, and thy God my God" (Ruth 1:16).

Sister Spafford has always been obedient to the priesthood leadership of the Church. President Lee, President Kimball, and President Tanner have all shared that information with me at different times. As a Relief Society general board we always knew that if we did what Sister Spafford asked us to do we would be obeying the leaders of the Church. And that, my sisters, is a marvelous blessing.

I know that Sister Spafford has traveled the length and breadth of the earth while proclaiming the truths of the gospel of Jesus Christ and upholding righteous womanhood and righteous endeavors. Her people are all of the good people of the earth. Her God is he who created the heavens and the earth. He is the same God who led the prophets of olden days and our beloved prophets today—he who dwells in the heavens, whose eyes are upon all people. He has been her bulwalk and her strength. And so I say, "Intreat me not to leave thee, or to return from following after thee: for whither thou goest, I will go . . . thy people shall be my people, and thy God my God."

It is a privilege to follow a noble woman who has followed other such women, the great women who have led the Relief Society, from Emma Smith to Amy Brown Lyman.

I must mention now another great and noble woman. She loved Relief Society. She worked in it all the days of her adult life. This woman of whom I speak loved her family; she lived the gospel of Jesus Christ and was a marvelous example to me. She was my mother. I would like to share one sacred experience with you.

When I took her to the hospital as she was suffering with an aneurysm she said to me, "Barbara, don't feel too badly if I die and don't let Daddy." I said, "Oh, Mother, don't talk like that." Her tenderness and care were evident as she said, "I'm not afraid to die. I know the plan of life and salvation and I have lived my life the best way I have known how to live."

I can think of no greater knowledge for any woman than to know the plan of life and salvation. By exemplifying that sure knowledge she is able to leave her children the greatest of all gifts.

I know that my mother gained much of her knowledge of the gospel of Jesus Christ from Relief Society. She increased her intelligence there and learned to live according to God's plan as she associated with her Relief Society sisters. Relief Society is intended to do this for all women, because the Prophet Joseph Smith said, "I now turn the key in your behalf in the name of the Lord, and this Society shall rejoice and knowledge and intelligence shall flow down from this time henceforth." (*History of Relief Society 1842-1966* [Relief Society General Board, 1966], p. 21.)

May we each be blessed with the knowledge and intelligence that Relief Society can bring into our lives.

May each of us live in such a way that other women will say of us as Ruth did of Naomi and as I say of Sister Spafford, "Intreat me not to leave thee."

May we recognize Jesus Christ as the perfect example. When we have a sure knowledge of his plan of life and salvation, nothing should intreat us to leave him.

May we go to our homes, to our wards, and to our stakes united as sisters and rejoice in this great Relief Society organization that the Lord has organized to bless his daughters. I humbly ask him to bless me in this great responsibility and to bless each of you.

I

Of Life and Love

1
Love Life

In a meeting one evening I heard the conducting officer call on a sister to sing for us extemporaneously. I was unprepared for what happened next. A young woman stood in the audience and made her way to the aisle; more accurately, she struggled to the aisle. There was no easy, graceful movement of her young body—it was twisted and her movements were laborious. She had been crippled by an encounter with polio early in her life.

I watched her come down the aisle and I wondered how she felt with every eye upon her tortured movement. It's a long walk from the audience to the stand for anybody called to perform, but for her it must have seemed like an eternity.

When she took her place on the stand, there was an audible sound of approval as she said that she would sing: "O That I Were an Angel." Then she laid her hand crutches down and straightened herself as tall as her twisted body could stand, and she began to sing:

> O that I were an angel, and could have the wish of mine heart,
> that I might go forth and speak with the trump of God,
> with a voice to shake the earth, and cry repentance
> unto every people! (Alma 29:1.)

The notes were clear and sweet and soaring. I felt transported. After the meeting I talked with this young woman. My heart was enlarged once more. She loved life—she of the deformed body, she who had been the victim of a crippling disease before she had had much chance at life. She told me that she was glad to be alive, that she loved the Lord, that she wanted desperately to serve him, and that she wanted to make her time on earth full of meaning.

As she turned from me, I watched her descend the three stairs and walk down the aisle to the host of friends that gathered to congratulate her on her inspiring performance. It sobered me and made me thoughtful.

In today's world, where so many find no hope, goodness, truth, beauty, or purpose, it was almost startling and certainly very refreshing to find one who wanted to live, who was grateful to be alive, who wanted to be of service to others, and who was making her life count. My mind went back to a time when I was much younger and I heard a double male quartette sing the song "I Love Life":

> I love life, and I want to live,
> To drink of life's fullness,
> Take all it can give.
> I love life; every moment must count.
> (Irwin Cassel)

The power of the message of this song welled within me as I felt the young woman's love of the gospel of Jesus Christ obviously guiding her. She loved life; she wanted to live, and make every moment count.

To be alive is an unparalleled opportunity for growth and development. Life in mortality offers an unprecedented privilege to fill the full measure of one's creation. It is an adventure that will never come again. The very excitement of life should set our spirits soaring.

There is an urgent need for each of us to love life, to live fully, and to reject the multiple philosophic views that relegate us to an existence filled only with tedium, never-ending nothingness, devoid of hope.

No one should accept any despondent view of mortality. Eternal progress is linked to this sojourn on earth where the spirit is subject to the flesh. Mortality allows each individual the opportunity to learn to walk by faith, to use his or her agency to choose right from wrong. That is why we are here. We cannot, in good conscience, write this experience off with a negative, dejected, unresponsive waiting out of time.

Like Cervantes's Man from La Mancha we should "dream the impossible dream" and "fight the unbeatable foe." It is the only way to really combat the tired cynicism that human error breeds.

Life is not always without trials. There are problems and there will continue to be problems, but the most significant thing each of us can do is to be confident that if we have faith in our Heavenly Father and live the best way we know how, he will direct us.

All of mortality is the time given for us to learn to choose right from wrong. This earthly period is for us to find the gospel and then to seek earnestly to understand our relationship with our Heavenly Father.

Victoria Lincoln once wrote: "How often, still, we approach the art of life like a pianist who sits by his locked piano and says with satisfaction, 'Today I have not struck one false note.' "

That surely is the antithesis, the direct opposite, of gospel teaching. One cannot sit complacently by and let talents lie unused, nor hope abilities will be developed without effort. One great pianist played before an audience in a sacrament meeting. He explained that the perfection of his performance took many years to develop and could be maintained only by his continuing to practice each day.

The gospel instructs us to develop our talents and to strive continuously for their perfection. It is of little concern if we make an honest mistake as we try to do so. Mistakes are a part of learning. The greatest tragedies come only when we willfully do what we know is wrong or if we do nothing at all.

The parables of Jesus point out our responsibility to enlarge our talents. The scriptures make it very clear that only our very best efforts will be acceptable to the Lord. "If thou doest well, shalt thou not be accepted? and if thou doest not well, sin lieth at the door" (Genesis 4:7).

We are each responsible for doing all we can do to develop the talents given us by the Lord. He wants us to rejoice in the gifts he bestows on us. We are often reminded that we must continue in learning and improving ourselves until the very end of our mortal lives.

For this reason the Lord has given us a church to provide occasions for ongoing learning and for organized opportunities to give service. One of the purposes of the Relief Society is to make available to women experiences from which they can learn and grow through participation.

Gamaliel Bailey said it well: "We live in deeds, not years; in thoughts, not breaths; in feelings, not in figures on the dial. We should count time by heart-throbs. He most lives who thinks most, feels the noblest, acts the best." (*The International Dictionary of Thoughts* [Chicago: J. G. Ferguson Publishing Company, 1969], p. 441.)

Circumstances and situations in our lives will change, but true principles will not. It is our greatest responsibility to learn and live by truth in whatever situation we find ourselves.

It is important to take on the task of living in today's world with real joy. We should look at mortal life as the time to be up and doing—learning and giving must go hand in hand if love and joy are to follow.

The gospel is good news. It is a gospel of truth. Pain comes when we err, so we must try to dedicate our best efforts to learning and living according to the truth we have. We should pray for more truth each day, especially the great truths embodied in understanding the sacred nature of life. Being born in today's world is a precious opportunity. We should never belittle our options; we have more than any who have ever lived before us. We must preserve what is good and true from the past and move forward with confidence to the challenge of loving life.

2

"Love Is Life, and Life Hath Immortality"

"Love," Emily Dickinson wrote, "is life, and life hath immortality." (*Love Poems and Others* [New York: The Peter Pauper Press]. p. 26.) Though no one ever really knows exactly what is in the poet's mind, there is a special thought suggested in these words that is universally recognized as truth. Life without love has a peculiar, haunting quality of resignation and stagnation about it. But love is a force that makes life volatile, and the contagion of it sweeps like wildfire from heart to heart. Where love is, life begets life and love begets love, and in all its compounding there is born a quality of immortality.

For example, think of the very touching scene in the popular Broadway musical *Carnival* in which Lili, the leading lady, is found up on the high diver's platform. She is very discouraged with life and feels so alone that she has determined to jump to her death. Paul, the puppeteer, seeing her, goes behind the puppet show stand, opens the curtains, and begins to talk to her through his puppets. He persuades her to come down from the dangerous height and charms her over to his stand, still using the puppets.

She talks to them and pours out her lonely heart. "No one loves me," she says. The puppets say, "But Lili, I love you, I love you. I love you and I love you." At last Paul comes from behind the puppet stand and says, "and I love you, Lili."

Into this poignant setting comes the lovely melody, "Love makes the world go 'round . . . Love makes the world go 'round and 'round and 'round . . ." 'Round and 'round into immortality.

Let me tell you one of my favorite true love stories. I learned about the story very late in its development. One night I went with my husband to a company dinner party. I sat next to an older man and his wife. She had suffered a stroke that severely handicapped her. He would frequently lean over to cut her meat. He literally fed her most of the food she ate. His manner was tender and very solicitous. As the meal finished he turned toward me with a sigh. I said, "You are so good to your wife."

"Why shouldn't I be? I love her," he replied.

He became very reminiscent and told me how they met, something of their courtship, and a little of their life together. "The first time I saw her," he said, "was at a party in Canada. She was giving a reading. I was taken by her beauty and talent and charm; she had long golden curls and wore a lovely white eyelet dress with a blue satin sash. I told my mother that I was going to marry her. My mother laughingly indulged me."

He continued, "I went on my mission and when I came home she was engaged to another. My bishop asked me to go to Salt Lake City on a special assignment. When I protested he told me that if I would always put the work of the Lord first I would find that the Lord would always take care of me. So, I made the long trek. When I got back she had broken her engagement. We dated and later we were married."

His wife rarely accompanied him out in public after that dinner. It wasn't long until her condition worsened and she was completely bedridden and virtually unable to speak. He was a General Authority and had his regular stake conference assignments. He visited and counseled the Saints week after week. It was his practice to add interest to her day and involve her in his activities by telling her all about the conferences. One day as he finished he teased: "If you are not going to talk to me then I'm not going to tell you about my experiences. You must not love me

any more." Tears welled up in her eyes and with great effort she
rallied enough strength to form the words "I do love you." It was
laborious and extremely slow but with great effort she got the
words out. He determined he would never again treat their love
lightly, for the love they knew transcended even the crippling
hindrance of her physical impairments.

At the funeral of this very special woman, Zina Card Brown,
every speaker commented on her love for her sweetheart, President Hugh B. Brown, and for others. Elder Marvin J. Ashton declared, "Some of us are where we are because of her." President
Marion G. Romney said, "Wherever she was she was a loving
lady." President N. Eldon Tanner declared that President Brown
was so successful because of her love. President Spencer W.
Kimball said that the love of President and Sister Brown was such
that they would be united together again everlastingly. They all
acknowledged that her love pulled them toward immortality—a
beginning of eternity.

A. J. Cronin wrote about another kind of love when he told of
the doctor of Lennox as the most unforgettable character he had
ever met. His, too, was a love that made the world go 'round. Dr.
Cronin describes this good doctor as "a simple soul who had no
wish to dominate an empire, but set out instead to conquer circumstances—and himself."

Dr. Cronin first knew this doctor as a boy. He calls him
"small, insignificant and poor." He hung on to a select band of
adventurous youths in the town of Levenford in Scotland, by the
skin of his teeth—barely accepted by them. The boy was lame—
so lame that he had to wear a boot with a sole six inches thick.
The minister's son called him "Dot and Carry" for the way he
limped along as he ran. That was shortened to "Carry."

Carry was shy, with a smiling continuing cheerfulness, and
this the boys mocked as they ran away from him. Carry's clothes
were patched and mended by his mother, "a gaunt little widow of
a drunken loafer," who supported herself and her son by scrub-
bing out shops. Carry supplemented the family income by getting
up at five o'clock every morning to deliver milk, and this often
made him late for school. The headmaster was more sadistic than

sympathetic and he would embarrass the lad unmercifully. Such
public embarrassments brought out Carry's stuttering.

His mother had set her heart on her son's becoming a minister, and so it was that Carry—who would have preferred being
outdoors in the woods and the moors with the wild things—found
himself studying for the ministry. He had an unusual knack of
healing, and was at last licensed to "cure souls."

But his first public sermon was a disaster. His carefully prepared words died as the terrible stammering took hold of him. His
poor mother mercifully was taken by an apoplectic seizure, and
after the funeral Carry disappeared from Levenford.

Carry drifted to teaching in a wretched school in the mining
district. Next he surfaced as a student of medicine at the age of
thirty. After his medical training he disappeared again.

Some time later Doctor Cronin and another of his boyhood
friends—now a Member of Parliament and a professor of
anatomy—went to the Highlands for a fishing holiday in the little
town of Lennox. The landlady at their inn was unpleasant and ill-
tempered. A couple of days after their arrival she slipped and
injured her knee. The two doctors offered their help but she refused it—only her own village doctor, whose skills she praised to
the skies, was going to care for her knee.

When that doctor arrived, he quickly reassured the patient and
then confidently and competently did his healing work. Then he
turned to the two visitors, and they discovered it was Carry; not
the former insecure, poorly dressed Carry, but a quietly self-
assured, successful country doctor. Recognition was instanta-
neous, and he invited the two men to his home for supper. There
they found Carry had a fresh and pretty wife and three children.
There were two other guests.

> Now, at his own table, he was a man poised and serene, holding his
> place as host with quiet dignity. His friends, both men of substance,
> treated him with deference. Less from what he said, than what was
> said by others, we gathered the facts. His practice was wide and scat-
> tered. His patients were country folk, canny, silent, hard to know.
> Yet somehow he had won them. Now as he went through the village
> the women would run to him, babe in arms, to consult him in the
> roadway.

There were other tales—of midnight vigils when in some humble home the battle for human life was waged: a child, choking with diphtheria, a plowman stricken with pneumonia, a shepherd's wife in painful labor, all to be sustained, comforted, exhorted, brought back haltingly, their hands in his, from the shadows.

The doctor was a force now, permeating the whole countryside, wise and gentle, blending the best of science and nature, unsparing, undemanding, loving this work he had been born to do. Conscious of the place that he had won in the affections of the people, Carry was a man who had refused defeat and won through to victory at last." (A. J. Cronin, "The Doctor of Lennox," *The Reader's Digest 20th Anniversary Anthology* [Pleasantville, N.Y.: The *Reader's Digest* Association, 1941].)

Love was life for Carry. His love literally meant life for others and for himself a renewed life.

There is something in the love that President Brown offered to his wife and she gave back to him that is very like the love the doctor of Lennox offered the people of his Scottish town and the love they gave back to him. Both first gave and then received love.

It is this love of which the scriptures speak. It is the eternal, life-giving force that permeates the universe and governs the heavens and the earth. It makes the weak strong and lifts people over and around the great boulders of difficulties that fall in life's paths from time to time.

During the last week of his earthly ministry the Lord Jesus Christ was approached for the third time by the Pharisees in an attempt to confound him. One of them, a lawyer, asked:

Master, which is the great commandment in the law?

Jesus said unto him, thou shalt love the Lord thy God with all thy heart, and with all thy soul, and with all thy mind.

This is the first and great commandment.

And the second is like unto it, Thou shalt love thy neighbor as thyself.

On these two commandments hang all the law and the prophets. (Matthew 22:36-40.)

This is the same teaching that has been given in each dispensation. Over and over again in every period of time the Lord has repeated this core instruction to his children. Sometimes he says that if we do not have love, then it doesn't matter what else we know or do. At other times he says, "If ye love me, keep my commandments." But always he stresses that the very heart of the gospel is to love God and man. "By this shall all men know that ye are my disciples, if ye have love one to another" (John 13:35).

After spending a lifetime studying and writing about men and events, Will Durant, the famous historian, was ninety-two years old when he was asked by a reporter what he could say that would distill more than two thousand years of history into one simple sentence.

The message Mr. Durant chose was: "Love one another. My final lesson of history is the same as that of Jesus," he said.

Durant added with a laugh: "You may think that's a lot of lollipop but just try it. Love is the most practical thing in the world . . . if you take an attitude of love toward everybody you meet, you'll eventually get along." (Pam Proctor, *Parade Magazine*, August 6, 1978, p. 12.)

It is interesting to read the references to love in the scriptures and find that the Lord explains that to love God is simply to do good and kind things to all of his children.

Could we take the time to really know those in our neighborhoods, to know them individually, their wants and needs and goals? Could we be responsive to them?

If we would give love we must be appreciative, long-suffering, patient, kind, humble. What are the qualities we need in order to receive love? Openness, receptivity, vulnerability, and humility. Are they practical? Can we really incorporate in today's world all of the laws of love given by Jesus? This is a question often asked; the answer is an individual commitment of faith and love. These commandments are practical, day-to-day guides to our behavior if we determine to make our own actions conform to them.

Loving people hasn't been tried very often in the world of international relations, and it is rare even in the world of national affairs. But at least one very notable experience comes to mind. Gandhi was the man who led India to her independence. He realized that turning the other cheek and returning good for hateful deeds would unloose great powers for his people.

One distraught Hindu man came to Gandhi in his suffering. His son had been killed by the Moslems. In retaliation he had taken the life of a small boy. Heavy-hearted he sought comfort from Gandhi, who told him he could find relief if he would find an orphaned Moslem boy and raise him as his own. But he was to raise him as a Moslem, not a Hindu. There is a sacrificing in love —a sacrificing that brings immortality. Gandhi suffered a great deal, but through his efforts ultimately millions of people were granted more freedom. Only the assassin's bullet cut his life short. One wonders what he might have contributed further in the development of the new nation had he lived.

One evening as I conversed with President Harold B. Lee, I said to him, "President Lee, you seem different some way . . ." He smiled and said, "You know what it is, don't you?" I shook my head and said that I really didn't know. Then he shared with me this remarkable experience.

"After I became the President of the Church I had a great desire to know what the Lord wanted me to do. One night, while I was sleeping, President David O. McKay came to me in a dream. He pointed his finger and looked at me with those piercing eyes of his, as only President McKay could do, and he said: 'If you would serve the Lord you must love and serve his children.' I awakened with a compelling desire to learn all I could about love so that I might serve the Lord. After I had read everything the scriptures had to say about love, I began more fully to put into practice all that I had gleaned from my study. That's what you can feel. It is my newfound ability to truly love and serve his children."

I watched President Lee even more closely that night and noted that not one person who came to the table to shake his hand left without receiving a special word of encouragement or an extra question that indicated the concern of the prophet. No one went away without seeing his smile or hearing his words of love.

I have thought of his wonderful example many times as the years have come and gone. President Lee is not with us now, but the spirit of that love which he exemplified still lives in my memory. He has helped me to understand what Orson Pratt meant when he said, "The children of Zion love in proportion to the heavenly knowledge which they have received; for love keeps pace with knowledge, and as the one increases so does the other, and when knowledge is perfected, love will be perfected also." (*The Seer*, p. 156.) We see this, also, in the life of our beloved prophet Spencer W. Kimball. Love has long been part of his life even before he became the President of the Church.

A stake president in Logan, Utah, kept a guest book, and after he passed away, that book was given to his son. When the son thumbed through the pages, he was very impressed with the signatures that were there. Most of the General Authorities had signed the book. One entry he saw was:

> Name: Elder Spencer W. Kimball
> Date: *1954*
> Position or Title: Apostle
> Hobby: "I love people."

He thumbed through many more pages and then he saw an almost identical entry ten years later:

> Name: Elder Spencer W. Kimball
> Date: *1964*
> Position: Apostle
> Hobby: "I love people."

We know President Kimball as a man of love. He thinks of love as a way to overcome even unknown offenses. Such an incident occurred with one of his neighbors. The man had been in the habit of going over to talk to President Kimball whenever he saw him in the yard. One day the neighbor's wife said, "You mustn't do that. The only time President Kimball is alone is when he is in the yard and then you go over and impose yourself upon him." After that the neighbor stayed in and just watched President Kimball through the window. A few weeks passed and then President Kimball rang this neighbor's doorbell and handed him a casserole.

"What's this for?" the neighbor asked.

"I don't know," replied President Kimball. "I've come to make amends for whatever I've done to offend you. You never come and visit any more so I decided I must have done something wrong."

It is President Kimball who has so lovingly explained to us that the Lord whispers to our hearts to go and do, and in this way he answers the fervent prayers of others. President Kimball says the Lord has chosen this method of answering prayers because he knows it is the way we will learn most effectively to give love.

I feel certain that such was the case cited by President S. Dilworth Young. Once, while caring for his wife, President Young observed, "When I had responsibility for an invalid, a good woman announced, 'I am coming to your house every Friday night from six until ten. You can count on it, so plan to go at six and find relief for those four hours.' How blessed she was to me! How good! She blessed both me and the invalid by new cheer, new smiles, new ideas."

Another example came to me by way of a letter from a sister in Medford Oregon Stake:

> I always thought I knew what compassionate service was. I've heard enough about it and I've been involved in it myself from time to time. I even introduced young girls to it and watched with pleasure how it changed their lives. I never thought it was . . . a big deal when I was asked to help by taking in meals, tending children, doing something to help. I often felt guilty reporting any compassionate service hours because it seemed like I had done so little, and usually I received happiness from it.
>
> Fifteen months ago I was stricken with a muscle-degenerating disease, and I have spent eleven and a half months as a hospital patient. Now compassionate service means so much to me. Oh, believe me, it's no little thing . . . for the "little" things that people do for others, are generally mountainous to the receiver. Compassionate service means love to me now.
>
> It is the hug and kiss from the tender heart of one that hasn't seen

you for some time, one who truly misses you. It's the one who can't
control her tears when she sees you in pain. Compassionate service
is the love of one who senses your need for companionship, so she
sits quietly and holds your hand until you fall asleep. It's the one
who telephones on her lunch hour just to say, "I love you, and I'm
praying for you." Oh, yes, and it's the one who brings you a bulletin
from church each week because she knows how lonesome you are
for those brothers and sisters you love.

Compassionate service that used to be such a small thing now is
one of the biggest things in my day. Having someone stay with me
each day for a period of time often makes the sisters feel guilty if I
don't have something for them to do. You see, they don't have any
idea how much just being with them means to me. I know they put
off routine duties, sometimes even urgent ones, just to listen when I
need to talk. They come to see me faithfully, and bring so much
cheerfulness into the room that it's impossible to be discouraged.
Their compassionate service includes "little" things like being alert
enough to help me move my legs when it's an obvious struggle
without making me ask for help—that saves me some self-respect.
It's also using a tissue to dry my tears and then pretending not to
have even noticed the tears. Again, that often helps me keep my self-
respect. Then on other occasions, it comes in the gentle persuasion
that lets me cry and get it all out.

See what small, insignificant things make up compassionate service? Small and insignificant? Only to the loving one on the giving
end. I speak from experience when I say there's nothing small to the
receiver about the love that accompanies compassionate service.

The compassionate service that is rendered is the evidence of
things not seen. It means that we actually believe in the teachings
of Jesus. Since its beginning Relief Society has tried to carry out
the sacred charge to do the work that Jesus did, and so the Relief
Society story is a story of love with myriads of instances of organized compassionate service throughout the wards and branches,
stakes and districts of the Church.

I was recently made aware of two visiting teachers who did all
of the grocery shopping for a homebound sister for over a year.
Then when she needed to have her blood pressure taken daily
they willingly assumed that responsibility as well.

In another ward the Relief Society sisters were organized to be there when the husband was out of the home and unable to care for his wife, a native of Thailand, whose English language skills were very limited. She had a disease that attacked every organ of her body. The sisters learned to use the respirator; they bathed her, combed her hair, brushed her teeth, straightened her house, and prepared meals as well. I heard this woman cry words of gratitude for the love and patience of those who served her.

After the first year of the Relief Society's existence, Eliza R. Snow, the secretary, wrote: "We hope the ladies of the Society will feel encouraged to renew their exertions, knowing that the blessings of the poor are resting upon them: We feel assured from what has passed under our personal observation, that many during the inclemency of the winter were not only relieved, but preserved from famishing through their instrumentality. More has been accomplished than our most sanguine anticipations predicted, and through the assistance and blessings of God, what may we not hope for the future?" (*History of Relief Society*, p. 23.)

We are now in that future Sister Snow spoke of. The work of love begun by that one little band of women is being carried forth in ten thousand bands of women in eighty-two countries. Like those sisters in Nauvoo, they are teaching the concepts of love and of charity by precept and example. Besides individual acts, they are organizing long-term programs of assistance to each other as need occurs and they are giving sustenance to neighbors both in and out of the Church.

Early in my administration, a Relief Society group from one of the BYU wards came to my office and presented me with a long scroll on which were listed the names of those who had completed the New Testament, the adult scripture reading course for that year. That Relief Society unit had determined that they would not only commit themselves to completing the Church reading assignment, they would live it and make it part of their lives. They wept as they told me that one girl who wanted very much to participte was blind and so each member of their Relief Society unit took a turn reading the scriptures to her so that she could participate in the project. Another girl became ill and so they all helped her keep up with her class assignments so that she could do her scripture reading as well.

They identified a second list and said so many problems came up that this group was not able to finish the scripture reading by the date they had set but they said, "You can be assured that they will complete it and that they are living what they are learning."

There is great value in combining efforts to motivate Relief Society members to go beyond theory into life-enriching experiences.

The love that brings the world life is the love that Jesus taught. It creates life in marriages, life in families, life in neighborhoods, communities, nations, and in the world. We must love the Lord and trust in his word. Love and trust will lead us into life eternal.

The little things we do for each other bring tenderness and joy into our day-to-day lives. They make life worth living.

The loving things we do for those who have despitefully used us bring even more love into our lives. They stop the perpetuation of hate and add to the component of good. The power of love is generative. I think my young daughter understood this when she was only three.

One morning I stepped to our back door to see the children off to school. Our little three-year-old daughter followed the children to the edge of the yard and watched them as they cut across the grass of a new neighbor. Enraged, the neighbor called out, "Don't you kids ever cut across my lawn. Don't you dare step one foot on it again." He couldn't see me but I could surely hear him and so could every other mother that was out to see her child off to school. As sweetly as three-year-olds can talk, ours turned to this angry neighbor and said, "You can step on our lawn if you want to." The next day that neighbor came out with a big smile and a darling teddy bear and he gave it to our little girl. There was never again a problem over that lawn.

Perhaps you will remember the story of Corrie Ten Boom, a fifty-year-old single woman who became a militant heroine of the anti-Nazi underground during World War II. The book is called *The Hiding Place*. It describes "an extraordinary adventure in Christian courage."

She recounts two examples of how love worked in her life to help her do good when she had been extremely ill-used. The first came was when she was a young woman in Holland. She was very much in love and had thought her love was returned. Then one day the young man came to her door with another young woman. He wanted to introduce Corrie to his fiancée. The family rallied around to help her face this crisis. After the young couple left, Corrie fled to her bedroom where she lay sobbing. Shortly her father came to her. His words were wise.

"Corrie, do you know what hurts so very much? It's love. Love is the strongest force in the world, and when it is blocked that means pain.

"There are two things we can do when this happens. We can kill the love so that it stops hurting. But then of course part of us dies, too. Or, Corrie, we can ask God to open up another route for that love to travel. . . . Whenever we cannot love in the old, human way, Corrie, God can give us the perfect way."

Later, after the terrifying experiences of a wartime Nazi concentration camp, she found herself face to face with a man who had been one of the SS guards there. Though she had just preached at a church service, seeing him brought back to her the horrors of the camp and the callousness of the jailers. Now however he was polite and smiling as he thanked her for her message—"To think that, as you say, He has washed my sins away."

He had offered her his hand, but she did not accept it. Anger and resentment pulsed through her even as she recognized her own sin in entertaining these feelings. "Jesus had died for this man. Was I going to ask for more?" Silently she prayed for the power to forgive and to be forgiven. Finally the prayer was answered.

> As I took his hand the most incredible thing happened. From my shoulder along my arm and through my hand a current seemed to pass from me to him, while into my heart sprang a love for this stranger that almost overwhelmed me.
>
> And so I discovered that it is not on our forgiveness any more than on our goodness that the world's healing hinges, but on His.

When He tells us to love our enemies, He gives, along with the command, the love itself." (*The Hiding Place* by Corrie Ten Boom with John and Elizabeth Sherrill [New York: Bantam Books], pp. 44-45, 238.)

That, you see, is what love is. It is the investiture, the immersing of ourselves in the lives of others and watching that change us and our surroundings.

I know that love is the life-giving force that renews the spirits of men and women and brings a new life to the world, life that moves us onward toward immortality.

The French scientist Pierre Teilhard de Chardin observed, "Someday, after we have mastered the winds, the waves, the tides, and gravity, we will harness for God the energies of love: and then, for the second time in the history of the world, man will have discovered fire." How wondrous!

We must learn to think of love as the great and powerful force that it is. Let us take the Lord's teachings about love very literally and work at mastering the skill of giving and receiving love. Love is the force by which we can renew the world. Surely, as the poet said, "Love is life, and life hath immortality."

3

Joseph Smith—A Life of Love

The Prophet Joseph Smith began his life like every other human being—a tiny, helpless infant, born of woman. What value had the life of one more baby? He came to the world the son of a farmer in a brand-new country. His mother was a religious woman, acquainted with the disputes between existing churches but with a firm faith in the Lord.

When his parents held him in their arms and decided to call him Joseph after his father, they did not know what his life would be. They knew his little body was free from crippling defect. They could tell he was an alert baby who could see and hear and cry.

I am sure his mother marveled a little at the wonder of her newborn child. Mothers do that, you know. They think the whole world should stop and take notice of God's latest miracle. But worlds seldom do that, and it is not likely that many besides the father, the other children, and those who came in to help with the birthing really stopped their daily work to take notice of the new child in the Smith home.

After all, Joseph Smith, Sr., was just one of many farmers trying to make his farm support his growing family. If you had asked his neighbors about him, they probably would have told you, "He's a hard-working sort of a fellow. He's had a run of bad luck, and he isn't getting rich very fast, but still he's a decent sort —someone you can count on, a good, solid citizen, from a good family."

And the baby's mother, Lucy—well, Lucy was a sister to that Major Stephen Mack of Revolutionary War fame, and her father, Solomon, had been a patriot too—good family. And she paid attention to her household. Her neighbors knew she taught her children how to read and to "figure," and she didn't neglect their Christian upbringing. They read the Bible and they could pray. Her children knew how to work. Lucy was a respectable New England housewife.

Little Joseph was more fortunate than some babies. He had a mother to keep him clean and warm and well fed and to sing him lullabies. Lullabies are a mother's way of passing on to her children her own dreams and aspirations. Maybe she sang to him of freedom in this new nation created by the Revolutionary War. After all, it was only 1805. The United States of America had only been free thirty years or so. It was still a bold new dream for mankind. Maybe she sang to him of the beauties of the world about them. They were people of the soil. They plowed the ground and planted the seed and lived by the springtime and harvest. Maybe when she worked a bubble out of his tummy and eased his discomfort, she patted him gently and told him about God and whispered to him of her own search for truth. Maybe when he grasped her finger and smiled at her from his safe place on her lap, she smiled a little and pulled him close to her and whispered, "Ah, Joseph, my little son, I love you."

I don't know that she did these things, but she might have. The record only tells us that Joseph Smith was born on the twenty-third day of December in Sharon, Windsor County, state of Vermont. He was the third son of Joseph Smith, Sr., and Lucy Mack Smith.

He passed those milestones of all babies: One day quite unexpectedly he rolled over, and then he sat up, and then he crawled, and then he pulled himself into a standing position. And the mother and the father and the other Smith children laughed with delight. They hastened to call each other as he took his first step, and they probably bragged a bit to their friends and neighbors when he formed his first words and sentences. Parents and families have been known to do things like that, too. At least, that's how it was in my family when my baby brother was born. He was adored. We called the whole family together whenever he took a step or added a new word. We cheered his every achievement and all seven of us reached out to catch him before he fell. The love a baby knows in a family of adoring brothers and sisters is warm and supportive and compounded, time and time again, to a force of immeasurable magnitude. That's how it was in our family and I think that's how it was in the Smith home, too, when Joseph came well and happy and full of the sweet joy of newborn life.

All in all, his growth from baby to little boy to a youth of fourteen was not particularly spectacular. His mother writes: "I shall say nothing respecting him until he arrived at the age of fourteen. However, in this I am aware that some of my readers will be disappointed, for I suppose, from questions which are frequently asked me, that it is thought by some that I shall be likely to tell many very remarkable incidents which attended his childhood; but, as nothing occurred during his early life except those trivial circumstances which are common to that state of human existence, I pass them in silence." (*History of Joseph Smith by His Mother* [Salt Lake City: Bookcraft, 1954], p. 6.) There was one exception.

He had just recovered from a two weeks' sickness known as typhus fever when he cried out with a severe pain in his shoulder. At first the doctor thought it was a sprain, and for two weeks the little boy suffered, gaining no relief from the liniment applied to his "sprain." The doctor came again, and this time he found a large fever sore that had gathered between Joseph's breast and shoulder. He lanced it, and the pain left the shoulder, but, to use Joseph's own words, "shot like lightning" down his side into the marrow of the bone of his leg. For two more weeks he suffered intense agony, and the leg swelled. His mother lovingly carried him about much of the time, hoping, as mothers do, to ease the pain a little by holding and rocking. But in this case the pain did not ease. At length this poor family had to send for the doctor again, and the leg was opened. This relieved the pain until the wound began to heal, then the pain became as violent as ever.

A council of surgeons was called, according to his mother's account, and these learned men decided that the boy's leg must be amputated to save his life. His mother said to the chief surgeon: "Dr. Stone, can you not make another trial? Can you not, by cutting around the bone, take out the diseased part, and perhaps that which is sound will heal over, and by this means you will save his life? You will not, you must not, take off his leg, until you try once more. I will not consent to let you enter his room until you make me this promise." (*History of Joseph Smith*, p. 56.)

Can't you just feel her heavy heart weeping for her little boy and praying for a miracle to save his leg? I can. I can hear the words of my Grandmother Mills insisting on one more try to save the leg of her daughter, my aunt. I can hear my own father describing the difficulties of adjusting to the loss of his leg, the problems of balance and acceptance of the loss once the leg was gone. And I can feel the pain in Joseph's mother's soul, caused by her growing, overwhelming awareness that she was helpless to relieve her little boy's lingering and intense suffering. From almost every woman's journal of that period comes the haunting cry of helplessness in the face of disease. Babies and children just slipped out of mortality and mothers grieved because they didn't know what to do; doctors didn't know what to do. I can feel the intense urgency in her body as she speaks to those men. She does not want to see him condemned to a cripple's life, but she does not want to see him slip away in death either. She knows he cannot be expected to bear much more pain. He has been so brave already. It has been weeks. And he is only seven years old.

The doctors who attended Joseph worked in very limited conditions for an operation of the magnitude they proposed. They would drill into the bone on either side of the diseased part and then chip out the badly infected area. This they would do to a small boy without anesthetic, for they had none. They wanted to tie him to the bed, but he would not be tied. They wanted to give him wine to dull his senses, but he would not take wine.

There can be no question of the love and confidence the boy had in his father, for he said to the doctor: "I will tell you what I will do—I will have my father sit on the bed and hold me in his arms, and then I will do whatever is necessary in order to have the bone taken out." (*History of Joseph Smith*, p. 57.) What a task for a loving father! Imagine the thoughts that ran through his mind as he sat down and gathered his suffering child into his strong arms, knowing what was about to happen.

There can be no question of the love Joseph had for his mother as he turned to her and said: "Mother, I want you to leave the room, for I know you cannot bear to see me suffer so; father can stand it, but you have carried me so much, and watched over me so long, you are almost worn out. Now, mother, promise me that you will not stay. The Lord will help me, and I shall get through it." (*History of Joseph Smith*, p. 57.)

She knew there was truth in what he said. In the seven long weeks that had passed she had tried desperately to ease his pain and suffering, and the ministrations had been night and day. She was worn out. No doubt she had insisted that she take the long night shift because her husband had to be about the farming. She had to take the long days by his side because she hoped that her being there would be a comfort. I think I have some idea what she thought about as she put some fresh, folded sheets under his leg. She probably kissed him or took his hand in hers in a last caress that said, "Courage, my son, and have faith." Quickly she turned and walked out of the room, out of the house, and away from his bedroom so that she could not hear the cries or the drill or anything.

I have tended the sick, and I have cried inside for the pain and suffering of my children. I know what happens when the heart is full of love. Tears come unbidden, and there is the helpless, hopeless ache. And, as in Lucy's case, there is the reality of God and the pleading for his comfort and care.

The screams were so loud that Lucy ran back from her place of refuge, and as she burst into the room, her little boy said, "Oh, mother, go back, go back." When the third piece of bone was taken, the cry was so loud and sharp that she burst in again and was forcibly pushed out of the room and kept out. When at last that ordeal was over, Joseph began to get better. He walked with a slight limp for the rest of his life, but he walked with his own leg.

The historian Richard Bushman says it took Joseph four years on crutches to get well after this operation. Finally, he could do without the crutches and walk using his leg again. Can you imagine the joy of that moment? The family may have been excited when Joseph took his first step as a baby, but I'm sure it didn't compare to the feeling of gratitude that came with his second "first" step.

Repeated crop failures drove the Smith family out of the state of Vermont and into New York. There in New York Lucy and Joseph Smith, Sr., started again with a new farm and a small four-room house with a lean-to bedroom. There were ten people in that little log cabin.

And it was from that house that Joseph walked one early spring morning in 1820. He went into a lovely grove of trees nearby and knelt down to pray. He had been concerned about the continuing arguments over religion in his neighborhood. Maybe the long illness had made him think about religious matters more, or maybe it was the poverty of their lives, or maybe it was local disputes about which was the right church, or maybe it was all these things together.

Anyway, he walked out of the family home and across the road and into the woods. There he knelt to receive the scriptural promise: "If any of you lack wisdom. . . ." He felt that he lacked wisdom particularly as it concerned God and man's relationship to Him.

So with a full trust that he had come to the only source of truth, this young boy on the verge of manhood knelt to ask which of all the churches that were recruiting him was the true church.

He had barely offered his prayerful request when thick darkness surrounded him, and he feared for his life. Then a pillar of light dispelled that awful gloom, and the light fell upon him. In the light were two personages. One of them called him by name and pointed to the other and said, "This is My Beloved Son. Hear Him!"

The young teenager looked and listened while the resurrected Christ spoke to him and told him to join none of the sects because "they teach for doctrines the commandments of men, having a form of godliness, but they deny the power thereof." (Joseph Smith—History 1:19.) The Christ instructed him in many things before the two heavenly beings withdrew into the heavens in a pillar of light.

Joseph picked himself up from the ground and walked back through the woods and across the road to his house. The answer to his prayer had been much more than he expected. It was not long after he came in the house that his mother knew something had happened. Mothers have a way of knowing when their children are profoundly moved. When our son was fourteen he too was given a special witness that God lived. He had gone to the Lord in pure faith asking for the promised witness, and the Holy Ghost verified to him that Jesus was the Christ. As he told me of the sacred experience there was no doubt in my mind. I could see the light that filled him as he told me of his spiritual witness. I never read Lucy's account of the experience her fourteen-year-old son had without feeling my heart beat a little faster. I can hear Lucy's concerned inquiry as she saw Joseph leaning there against the fireplace. He replied: "Never mind, all is well—I am well enough off. . . . I have learned for myself that Presbyterianism is not true." (Joseph Smith—History 1:20.)

When Joseph told a minister about his remarkable experience, that man was not interested. He was more than "not interested"; he greeted the boy's testimony with ridicule and characterized it as fraud. And so the persecutions began.

But inside the Smith home they believed. Joseph, the boy, had the confidence of his father and mother and the trust of his brothers and sisters.

In the years that followed Joseph's vision, he received other instruction from heavenly messengers. His mother gives this insight into what went on at home:

> Joseph continued to receive instructions from the Lord, and we continued to get the children together every evening for the purpose

of listening while he gave us a relation of the same. I presume our family presented an aspect as singular as any that ever lived upon the face of the earth—all seated in a circle, father, mother, sons and daughters, and giving the most profound attention to a boy, eighteen years of age. . . . We were now confirmed in the opinion that God was about to bring to light something upon which we could stay our minds, or that would give us a more perfect knowledge of the plan of salvation and the redemption of the human family. This caused us greatly to rejoice; the sweetest union and happiness pervaded our house, and tranquility reigned in our midst. (*History of Joseph Smith* pp. 82-83.)

I think it is significant that the Prophet Joseph had the strength of a warm and loving family circle to sustain him through the early persecutions. It is also an exceptional demonstration of his parents' love that they would both accept his visitation with faith and submit themselves to him for teaching. After all, they, as his parents, were charged from antiquity with the responsibility of loving and instructing their offspring. Even though he was barely out of childhood he challenged the whole structure of human contact with the divine. Yet those who knew him best and loved him most accepted his word. It was a very critical balance to the rage and the persecution that were beginning to come against him from the outside world.

Joseph went to Pennsylvania to take a job, and while there he met Emma Hale. There can be no question about the love these two shared. She was unable to obtain the approval of her parents, but being of age, she married him. She gave her whole life into his hands, and from the standpoint of her parents Joseph was not a very good risk, for they called him a "visionary" man, and they worried at the expressions of hostility and persecutions aimed at him.

Joseph and Emma found it necessary to leave home after home, and sometimes the moves were precipitated by severe persecution. Four out of the eight children born to them died at birth or shortly thereafter. Ugly, noisy men burst into their home and dragged Joseph forth to tar and feather and beat him. Facing trumped-up charges, Joseph was unjustly jailed or otherwise kept away from home time after time. All the things Emma's father had said about Joseph's lack of prospects for a stable home came true.

Still Emma loved Joseph. She believed in him. In the twenty-fifth section of the Doctrine and Covenants she was told by the Lord: "And the office of thy calling shall be for a comfort unto my servant, Joseph Smith, Jun., thy husband, in his afflictions, with consoling words, in the spirit of meekness." (Verse 5.)

There are many other important instructions in that section, and Emma was given tremendous responsibilities and opportunities. I doubt that she ever had a responsibility heavier or more important than comforting and consoling her beloved Joseph.

Emma was in Quincy, Illinois, on March 7, 1839, when she wrote the following letter to her husband, Joseph, who was imprisoned in Missouri:

> Having an opportunity to send by a friend I make an attempt to write, but I shall not attempt to write my feelings altogether, for the situation in which you are, the walls, bars, and bolts, rolling rivers, running streams, rising hills, sinking vallies and spreading prairies that separate us, and the cruel injustice that first cast you into prison and still holds you there, with many other considerations, places my feelings far beyond description. Was it not for conscious innocence, and the direct interposition of divine mercy, I am very sure I never should have been able to have endured the scenes of suffering that I have passed through, since what is called the Militia, came into Far West, under the ever to be remembered Governor's notable order; an order fraught with as much wickedness as ignorance and as much ignorance as was ever contained in an article of that length; but I still live and am yet willing to suffer more if it is the will of kind Heaven, that I should for your sake. (Joseph Smith Papers, Archives of The Church of Jesus Christ of Latter-day Saints, Salt Lake City, Utah.)

The letter goes on to say that Emma had sent a change of clothes with Heber C. Kimball, who had agreed to get them to the Prophet in jail.

We know of her suffering, for she writes this poignant sentence: "No one but God, knows the reflections of my mind and the feelings of my heart when I left our house and home, and almost all of everything we possessed excepting our little children, and took my journey out of the State of Missouri, leaving you shut up in that lonesome prison.''

She signs her letter, ''Give my respects to all in that place that you respect, and am ever yours affectionately.''

Emma provided him the love and comfort he required to sustain him through all of the persecutions. His brothers and sisters sustained him with love and trust not only in the beginning but throughout the entire time of his ministration. There can hardly be a more noble example of brotherly love than that left by Hyrum. And the Saints Joseph led loved him. Many visitors to Nauvoo commented upon the love he commanded from his people.

Stephen A. Douglas, the ''little giant'' of American political fame, remarked that if he could command the following of Joseph Smith, he would resign his seat in Congress and go out to Oregon. He said, ''In five years a noble state might be formed; and then if they would not receive us into the Union, we would have a government of our own.'' (Quoted in letter from Orson Hyde, *History of the Church* 6:373-74.)

The Prophet himself reported: ''Sectarian priests cry out concerning me, and ask, 'why is it this babbler gains so many followers, and retains them?' I answer, It is because I possess the principle of love.'' (*Teachings of the Prophet Joseph Smith* Joseph Fielding Smith, comp. [Salt Lake City: Deseret Book Company, 1938], p. 313.)

I have mentioned these facts about the Prophet's life because I want you to understand that although the Prophet knew bitterness and persecution, he also knew the warmth of much love. I think it was this experience with human love that helped him understand the divine law of love that God revealed to him. He gave love, and love came back to him. A major part of the restoration of the fulness of the gospel relates to helping us understand that love is an active force—a power from heaven. It is the power through which man may tap the resources of heaven.

In fact, the Prophet Joseph declared: ''Love is one of the chief characteristics of Deity, and ought to be manifested by those who aspire to be the sons of God. A man filled with the love of God is not content with blessing his family alone, but ranges through the whole world, anxious to bless the whole human race." (*Teachings,* p. 174.) The principle of love is evident in all of the major contributions the Prophet made.

Let me use the analysis of President Stephen L Richards (*Contributions of Joseph Smith* [pamphlet, 1969]) to show you what I mean.

First, the First Vision gives us a very clear and simple understanding of the nature of the godhead: the Father, the Son, and the Holy Ghost, three personages distinct and separate and possessed of feelings and characteristics such as mercy and compassion. No more need men struggle with the idea that God is an essence or a mere principle of force or power. God is a being. He can and does answer prayers. He does love and care.

Second, the Prophet explained the nature of the priesthood. The new concept is eloquently described in Section 121 of the Doctrine and Covenants: "The rights of the priesthood are inseparably connected with the powers of heaven, and . . . the powers of heaven cannot be controlled nor handled only upon the principles of righteousness" (verse 36); and then "No power or influence can or ought to be maintained by virtue of the priesthood, only by persuasion, by long-suffering, by gentleness and meekness, and by love unfeigned; By kindness, and pure knowledge, which shall greatly enlarge the soul without hypocrisy, and without guile" (verses 41-42).

President Richards comments: "Here is the genius of the government of Christ. No compulsion—just persuasion; no unrighteousness, or autocracy—only goodness and love. Here is the answer to the religious intolerance and crimes of the centuries; the complete refutation of the alleged injustice of God." (*Contributions,* p. 3.) Clearly the work of the priesthood is a work of love.

Third, the Prophet gave us a new concept of man, with an understanding of his past, present, and future. President Richards observes: "The continuity of intelligence and intelligences; the fatherhood, and motherhood too, of our individual spirits; the free agency and choice which were ours in the pre-earth life;

spiritual creation preceding mortal creation; the relationship of the body to the spirit in this life and in the hereafter, the transcendent scheme of eternal progression—all these and many related items constitute a unified, logical authoritative exposition without counterpart in Christian literature." (*Contributions*, p. 47.) An interlocking plan represents the most careful, loving contribution a godly Father could make to the eternal well-being of his children.

Fourth, the underlying philosophy of the Word of Wisdom brings us a far-reaching understanding of the body as the tabernacle of the spirit—part of an eternal plan. The revelation of the Word of Wisdom to the Saints was an act of love. In a day when medical research and knowledge were extremely limited, the Father of us all gave us information about our bodies that could only be a blessing to our physical well-being.

Fifth, the Prophet gave us a full understanding of the idea of the whole human family being the children of God. Through the Prophet, the Lord has established a theology that allows the universal justice and love of God to be operative. Resurrection will come to all, but exaltation is reserved for those whose obedience and works make them eligible.

Sixth, the Prophet revealed to us an understanding of the purpose of temples and the saving work for the dead that should go on there. Such work performed by the living for people they do not know is a pure act of love to make eternal progression possible for those who died without the law.

Seventh, the Prophet Joseph gave us an understanding of the sealing ordinances. "He sanctified the association of loved ones" (*Contributions*, p. 6), and by the restoration of the priesthood authority he brought to us an understanding of the eternal bonds of family association. President Richards points out: "He made the father a priest and the mother a priestess in the temple of the home. If his glorious interpretation of this divine institution could have general application, the ills of society would be cured and the brotherhood of mankind established." (*Contribution*, p. 6.) Many an early convert found the appeal of eternal relationship of compelling interest, for they wanted their love to continue.

Eighth, the organization of the Church is a great blessing to mankind because it provides an orderly way to fulfill the assignment given to those who believe. It provides an orderly missionary program to preach the glad tidings to all the world. And it provides an organization where we can give service to each other and convert ourselves to the power of loving service, where we can perfect ourselves, and where we can teach ourselves.

President Marion G. Romney once observed that the greatest contribution of the organization of the Church is to give the Saints an opportunity to learn to work with each other. The value of working together is that we learn to love one another.

Ninth, the Prophet's tremendous literary output has left us a great deal of light by which to live.

The Prophet's great contribution to our lives and to the general enlightenment of the world continues, and a careful examination of how to apply all the truth he revealed to us makes it clear that in the gospel are the answers to most of the world's great problems. Applying the law of love itself would make it possible for us to live in harmony and without poor among us.

It sounds so altruistic that many reject the idea as being idealistic and simplistic, when in actual fact it may be the most realistic and practical of all suggested solutions to human misery.

The law of love as Christ gave it in the meridian of time and as he reiterated it through Joseph Smith in the opening of the dispensation of the fulness of times is very simple: Love your neighbor as yourself; do good to them that despitefully use you; turn the other cheek; if compelled to go one mile, then go two.

Remember the story in the Old Testament of a ruler who had leprosy and wanted to be cured. Nothing could be done by the wise men and the healers. This ruler had a little servant girl from the Hebrews among his household, and she told him that there was a prophet of God who could heal him. So the ruler packed up his goods and wealth and went to see the prophet in the far-distant place. When he got there, the prophet told him to go down and bathe in the river Jordan seven times, and he would be cleansed. The ruler was incensed. He had better-looking rivers at home, and he could bathe there. He almost lost his chance at being healed because the method didn't appeal to him. But his servants prevailed on him to follow the prophet's counsel, and he was cured. (See 2 Kings 5.)

So too we have the light of the glorious principle of love, which the Lord has given us to help us help one another and make it possible for the world to live in peace. We turn our backs upon it and say it is not practical to solve human problems that way. But is there another way? The Lord's plan for relieving human suffering can be started by any one soul. It can be run for a lifetime without bureaucracy. It can relieve pain and suffering, starting with the first hour of commitment. There is no limit to the good that can be done if the heart is converted to the idea that we can apply the principle in our daily lives.

Now, about the contributions that Joseph Smith made to the lives of women both in the Church and out: The concepts which I have just outlined are basic to our understanding. They free our minds of ignorance regarding the interplay between God and man, and they open the vista of eternal progression to all of us.

The scriptures are given to man, male and female. I think it is significant that all of the saving ordinances of the gospel are for women as well as men. The freedom of truth, as revealed by the Prophet Joseph, has been available to all women. So has membership in the Church and the ecclesiastical vote.

Thus, one of the great blessings for Mormon women is the realization of truth. The heavens are opened, and God speaks again to mankind through his prophets. The light of truth cuts through the blackness of ignorance, and the whole plan of salvation is again available.

The early women of the Church testified that this was one of the most electrifying truths. They had prayed for such knowledge and direction, and when they heard the gospel, they knew they had found light again.

One conference time I had an opportunity to talk with women from a number of foreign countries. I asked them what the gospel meant to them, and the most frequent response was: "It has brought us love." And, they said, "It has made possible eternal marriage." One woman added: "You see, in my country the man may put his wife away for any cause, and the woman has no legal recourse. But the gospel teaches that marriage is for eternity. It introduced us to the concept of eternal love."

The clear exposition of the Prophet's work gives an understanding of the power of love and its critical importance in the plan of life and salvation. Each one may enter the place where God and Christ are if he has schooled himself well enough to live fully the law of love.

One new convert gathering to Nauvoo wrote, "The people here have such love one for another." The historian T. Edgar Lyon said that the City Beautiful, Nauvoo, was built because the people had love and trust for each other and they cooperated together in every needful way.

The Prophet Joseph Smith in his last public address told his people to remember that he loved them and would give his life for them. This he subsequently had to do, and when his lifeless body was brought back home again, the Saints lined the hot and dusty streets, and the lamentations were heart-rending.

My great-grandmother Smoot stood in the weeping crowd and saw the martyred Joseph and his brother Hyrum. She saw their grieving wives and their aged mother. She left us a record of that despairing moment and testified that all Israel mourned as they had never mourned before and as they have never mourned since. Lucy Mack Smith, the woman who gave birth to an infant son who grew up to be a prophet, left us her testimony that she seemed to hear her prophet son say, "Mother, weep not for us, we have overcome the world by love; we carried to them the gospel, that their souls might be saved; they slew us for our testimony, and thus placed us beyond their power, their ascendency is for a moment, ours is an eternal triumph." (*History of Joseph Smith*, p. 325.)

What do you think their mother felt as she heard that thought, "Weep not for us, we have overcome the world by love"? But the little boy she had held in her arms as an infant and had comforted in times of pain had grown and was now gone.

His message is with us yet. His message of love is an invitation to all to overcome the problems of this world. God grant us the courage and the faith to try the simple answer of love to complex problems and thereby invite all the power of heaven to be our strength.

II

Of Loving the Challenge
of Learning

4

The Powers Within

This is an exciting and challenging time in history. It is a time of great growth, great expectations, and of great needs for all people.

However, extreme viewpoints regarding women have become political and social issues. These conflicts make it important for each women to understand her magnificent potential, her irreplaceable contributions, her eternal destiny—and those of each man as well.

Challenges are not unique to our times. Look at the life of President Zina D. H. Young, the third general president of Relief Society. She was bright, observant, and deeply religious. Even so she suffered sickness, trials, tribulations, and sorrows. She witnessed the burning of the homes of the Saints in Nauvoo before the exodus. Her father and mother both died as a result of persecutions against the Mormons. She had two children by her first marriage. Then, later, she married Brigham Young and raised four of his children along with her two and the one daughter born to them.

President Brigham Young gave Zina the mission of establishing the silk culture in the territory of Deseret. The silkworms were extremely repugnant to her, but in spite of that she successfully completed the assignment.

Her love of the Lord and her determination to follow the direction given by the prophet made it possible for her to do what she was asked to do, and I am sure that she had to develop within her some special strengths in order to be able to do it. I can't tell you how grateful I am that I don't have to handle those silkworms.

Some time ago a beautiful young woman sent me a book entitled *Hope For The Flowers.* (Trina Paulus [Paramas, N.J.: Paulist Press, 1972].) As I read it, I thought, "It's too bad that Sister Zina Young didn't have this book. It might have given her some new insights about worms." Let me share its message with you.

It tells of a tiny striped caterpillar and how he joined a bunch of other squirming, pushing caterpillars who were trying to get to the top of a pile. It was only when he talked to a certain yellow caterpillar that the two of them decided that getting to the top wasn't really what they wanted most. So, they climbed down and away from the others. They enjoyed being together, they ate and grew fat, until one day they became bored and they wanted to find out if there was more to life. The striped caterpillar decided to find out by climbing again to the top of the caterpillar pile. The yellow caterpillar felt ashamed that she didn't agree but decided it was better to wait until she could take action she could believe in. So he climbed, and she wandered aimlessly until she saw a caterpillar hanging upside down on a branch, caught in some hairy substance. She said, "You seem to be in trouble. Can I help you?"

"No," said the hanging caterpillar, "I have to do this to become a butterfly."

"Butterfly? What is a butterfly?"

"It's what you are meant to become. It flies with beautiful wings and joins the earth to heaven. It drinks only nectar from the flowers and carries seeds of love from one flower to another. Without butterflies the world would soon have few flowers."

The yellow caterpillar exclaimed, "It can't be true! How can I believe there's a butterfly inside you or me when all I see is a fuzzy worm? How does one become a butterfly?"

The hanging caterpillar said, "You must want to fly so much that you are willing to give up being a caterpillar."

The yellow caterpillar began fearfully but continued the process until at length she became a butterfly. Then she helped the striped caterpillar learn to become what he was really meant to be.

Like the caterpillars who will one day become butterflies, we have the magnificent potential to develop the powers within us and become greater than most of us dare dream. "God has . . . made us the custodians of some great powers," said Elder Sterling W. Sill. (*The Power of Believing* [Salt Lake City: Bookcraft, 1968], p. 6.) We have the power and the capacity to perform so well that we can inherit all that our Father has if we begin the process and continue until we become what we are really meant to be.

Consider just three of the great powers of which you are custodians. Perhaps then you can begin to understand the process necessary to become what you are really meant to be.

First, you have great physical powers. Look at yourself; notice your hands, your arms, your legs, your feet, your face, your eyes, your ears, your mouth, and your nose. You must admit that you are a magnificent creation when you realize how intricate these components are and what you can do because of them. If by any chance there is more of you than you would like to see you can do something about that too. And, if you do, it will make a great difference in how you feel about yourself.

I was in Washington, D.C., where I met a woman in her thirties who has not yet married. She is stunning—tall, and full of enthusiasm. She is running an oil recycling business. This young woman told me about her recent campaign to lose weight. I think that she had taken off over forty pounds. "I can't begin to tell you what it has done for me," she said. "Having decided to reduce my weight and then having successfully done it has made it easier for me to relate to others because I feel so good about myself. It is exciting."

Her example serves to illustrate that physically we have the power to choose from the options available to us. We can keep the extra pounds or we can lose them. We can lose them by taking in fewer calories, or we may desire to put ourselves on a consistent program of exercise, or both. The point is that we have the power to lose weight and thereby increase our capacity to do what we want to do.

I like the statement made by Bryant S. Hinckley, father of President Gordon B. Hinckley: "When a man makes war on his own weaknesses he engages in the holiest war that mortals ever wage. The reward that comes from victory in this struggle is the most enduring, most satisfying and the most exquisite that man ever experiences. The power to do what we ought to do is the greatest freedom." (*That Ye Might Have Joy* [Salt Lake City: Bookcraft, 1958], p. 38.)

I hope at some time you will feel the reward of such a victory and that you will recognize the miracle of your mortal body in helping you to gain this newfound freedom.

B. H. Roberts said:

> Think for a moment what progress a man makes within the narrow limits of this life. Regard him as he lies in the lap of his mother . . . a new-born babe! There are eyes, indeed, that may see, but cannot distinguish objects; ears that may hear, but cannot distinguish sounds; hands as perfectly fashioned as yours and mine, but helpless withal; feet and limbs, but they are unable to bear the weight of his body, much less walk . . . and yet within the short span of three score years and ten, by the marvelous working of the wondrous power within . . . what a change may be wrought! From the helpless babe may arise one like unto Desmosthenes or Cicero, or Pitt, or Burke, or Fox, or Webster, . . . or from such a babe may come a Nebuchadnezzar, or an Alexander, or a Napoleon, who shall found empires or give direction to the course of history. (*The Mormon Doctrine of Deity* [Salt Lake City: Deseret News, 1903], pp. 33-34.)

The miracle of the mortal body became apparent to me one afternoon when I was holding my first baby. It was a girl, and suddenly she seemed to stop breathing. I tried to force air into her lungs. I cried to the Lord in desperation, and after only a few seconds that seemed like an endless hour, she began to breathe normally again. The problem was diagnosed as an enlarged thymus gland that needed treatment. I shall never forget how grateful I was for the miracle of life and for the power of the body that I knew that day. I determined to do my very best to help her use her life as the Lord intended when he gave her to me to care for and to love.

I know now the powers within these bodies, and I know they are the powers not only to create life but to live life in such a way that mortality will be a happy and meaningful experience.

When these miraculous systems malfunction—and maybe only then—we fully appreciate the complexity of the systems that give the body life. Only as we struggle to understand the body in order to treat the ailments it falls heir to in this life do we fully appreciate its remarkable nature and the intricate interrelationships that exist. The human body is most remarkable. It can walk, run, jump, climb, swim, ski, play, jog, and on and on, but not the least of its remarkable capabilities are its compensatory powers. We find these powers as we observe some of our friends and acquaintances—or even ourselves—who have birth defects, accidents, or illnesses that cause the functions we counted on to be lost so that other parts of the body have to substitute.

Curt was a good basketball player before his accident, but afterward he did not dwell on what his body could not do. When he had no legs, he trained his arms and built strength in them to compensate for his missing legs. Curt Brinkman broke some records in his wheelchair in the famous Boston Marathon. He had found other ways to use the powers within him and he became a champion.

Know the full joy of your mortal body. The power is within you to do an infinite variety of things. When one avenue of activity is denied by a physical impairment, there is still a rich variety of alternate choices available to you.

It is the masterful creation of our bodies that gives us these wonderful abilities because we are the literal offspring of our Heavenly Father. He, whose spirit children we are, organized these mortal bodies and provided us each with a powerful instrument capable of vitalized mortal living. However, Elder LeGrand Richards cautions: "There are many who think their bodies are their own and that they can do with them what they will, but Paul makes it plain that they are not their own, for they are bought with a price, and that 'If any man defile the temple of God, him shall God destroy; for the temple of God is holy, which temple ye are.' " (*A Marvelous Work and A Wonder* [Salt Lake City: Deseret Book, 1950], p. 380.)

We do have great physical powers within us to create life, to control our abilities and capacities, and to compensate for disabilities; and these physical powers require us to take good care of our bodies. At the very least we should obey the Word of Wisdom, eat properly, sleep and exercise regularly, and abstain from taking anything into our bodies that will destroy their powers, for we will be held accountable for them.

Consider your mental powers. Think of your infinite capacity to learn, your ability to control your attitude toward learning, and your ability to adapt to and draw from the happenings of each day. No mother can watch the progress of her child without being filled with wonder at his endless desire to learn. It is one of the joys of being a parent.

There are hungers and frustrations that accompany the young child's eagerness to grow and learn. Watch a child struggle to walk. Again and again he tries—up on his feet, down on the floor, bumps and hurts, cries of pain or frustration until at last he walks. At first he holds on to the offered hand for support, and then he pushes it away. A child must go through the process if he would grow and gain a sense of achievement.

This fundamental principle applies to every person if real learning is to occur. Each must reach out for strength from others, then struggle and stretch to the limits of his or her own capacities to feel the ultimate sense of achievement.

With that realization, look back over the centuries of mankind's experience in mortality and see the great learning that has come to us from others. I mentioned my trip to Washington, D.C. While there I had the opportunity to visit the National Air and Space Museum. It is a huge structure, housing all the tangible machines of flight that are part of our national legacy. Within those walls are housed many dreams. The history of man's conquest of the moon is documented there in countless projects and written records. It is just one of the tiny fragments of human inquiry that has yielded enormous amounts of knowledge.

In the earliest records of human desire to go to the moon are stories of drinking a magic potion and being wafted to the moon or harnessing giant birds that could pull a raft carrying a man to the moon. Some even thought about covering men with suction cups so that as the dew would evaporate from the cups the traveler could be lifted to the moon. Then came a reflection of man's technological progress with the thought of gliding, and finally it occurred to someone that a person might be shot by a rocket to the moon.

More than three hundred years ago the necessary principles of physics were beginning to be known, and Kepler declared that when we had developed the technology to build machines to go to the moon, men would come forward to ride those machines. They did, and the moon once whimsically described as being made of green cheese suddenly became a real place—barren, foreboding, made of rocks and boulders with no living thing on it.

In the process of conquering that distance to the moon, many things were discovered. As the hardware was developed to lift the rocket from the earth and hurl it through space, the first major discoveries with computers were made. From the room full of equipment it took to do the first computer calculations developed our present pocket calculators.

Walk the corridors of any great university and look into the libraries and the laboratories and you will find more projects, designed to overcome the ignorance and the unknown, than could have even been dreamed about a few short years ago.

Knowledge builds upon knowledge. There is no end to the capacity of men and women to learn. The great vision of the gospel is that we grow in wisdom and in knowledge and in favor with God and man. You must put yourself to that task because you have the power.

There is most often an urgent desire for knowledge in us when we are young. I smiled at my young grandson who, long before he went to school, would take science books to his mother and say,

"Read them to me." She would ask, "Don't you want to read a storybook?" He would reply, "No, Mother, I don't know anything about science, and I want to learn."

There are no handicaps that cannot be overcome.

I was told that when J. Willard Marriott returned home from a summer of working to pay for his last year of college, his father had bought a herd of three thousand sheep and wanted Bill to tend them. Despite his crushing disappointment at losing out on a year of schooling, he did what his father asked. But he took his college textbooks with him, and in the evenings after a hard day's work he studied on his own so that he would not fall behind. The sheep drive was successful, and the next year J. Willard Marriott graduated from the University of Utah.

Joseph Larsen, a fine stake president in Illinois, was injured while serving his country. The accident left him without the use of his legs, and confined to a wheelchair. But he, with the help of his lovely wife, went on to finish his education. He is now a Dean of Life Sciences at the University of Illinois. He is a spiritual giant among the brothers and sisters of his stake. The capacity to learn did not end when his ability to walk ended. He kept going.

A delightful sister, Ruth Knudson, took me on a tour through the National Gallery of Art. When her husband passed away, she decided that she would make good use of her time alone. She studied art history. It was so fascinating to her that she wanted to tell others about it so she began conducting tours. Now her life is rich and full as she continues to seek more learning about art in order to constantly teach others.

Continuing education is important for an enriched life. We can learn in so many ways. For example, one of my daughters was visiting with Sarah Stohl Boyer and observed that Sarah's little girl had a new and attractive braid in her hair. My daughter remarked on this lovely style and Sarah said that she would teach her how to do it. She commented, "When I realized how many years of combing and setting hair I would have with five little girls, I thought I might as well learn all I could about caring for hair, including a lot of different and charming hairstyles." I wonder why I didn't think of that. I had four daughters.

Another family keeps their learning alive by acquiring things like telescopes, looms, a potter's wheel, and a greenhouse. They accompany each new piece of equipment with an intensive study so that they can master new skills. Imagine the many happy, productive hours they spend together.

Classes are available, books are available; constant, never-ending media is available. All of these things can work to our good if we desire to continue learning. Once after I had returned from a trip to Mexico, I told President Spencer W. Kimball that I wished I could speak Spanish. His quick reply was, "Well, you can learn, can't you?"

At first I thought, "No, not at my age, I can't," and then I realized that of course I could learn. I haven't learned Spanish yet, but I know that I can. We all can come from the unknown to the known. We can develop skills, but we must remember that one of the significant tools for learning is our ability to control our own attitudes. All the knowledge in the world will not help us if we resist learning. There is no end to our capacity to learn if we apply ourselves diligently and eagerly to the task.

A slight change of attitude to a new point of view can open a whole new world to you. I can remember descending into the Los Angeles airport one day. I was seated next to a landscape architect. I was thinking about the myriad of houses and buildings below us when he looked across me and said: "Can you imagine how many sprinkler heads there are down there?" The landscape problems of a big city had never entered my mind before that, but occasionally I think about them now.

Perhaps the most important point regarding your intellectual powers is the fact that you have the power to grow from your day-to-day experiences. At one time or another you will have occasion to choose between a life of bitterness and a life of beauty. You have the power within you to make such a choice, and the Lord has promised that you can count on him for sufficient help to have an abundant life if you choose to live by the principles that lead you to personal growth and development.

Brother Marriott turned the circumstances that kept him from school into great personal discipline and a learning experience.

President Larsen accepted the accident that put his body in a wheelchair with courage and determination. He also developed a remarkable optimism that makes him stand tall in spirit and intellect even though his legs will no longer hold him upright. Sister Knudson accepted her situation and despite persisting loneliness receives abundant satisfaction as she is sought out for her deep insights into art treasures. This brings happiness to her and to others.

This great adaptive quality is part of the power within us that can shape our lives. We can make contributions with excellence if we so choose. When we use our mental powers wisely, we can more easily become what we are really meant to be.

There is another great power within you—the power for enormous spiritual growth and the infinite possibility for perfecting yourself. One way you can develop your spiritual power is by sharing the gospel, because the gospel has the principles upon which all growth is predicated. Once we understand those concepts we need opportunities both to teach them and to live them.

Another way to develop your spiritual power is to render acts of loving kindness and compassionate service. Such acts are of real value to us only when they are given out of personal choice, not pressure. Albert Schweitzer wisely said, "The only ones who will ever be truly happy are those who have sought to serve."

For example, my former bishop and his wife entered the Missionary Training Center to prepare for their mission to Nigeria; at the same time, their daughter also entered the Missionary Training Center to prepare for her mission to Peru. This family is well aware of the conveniences and luxuries they will give up, but they are eager to serve the Lord by loving and serving his children. The Lord wants us to be mindful of each other and to be dependent upon each other. For this reason he has distributed his gifts among us all, giving one to one and one to another so that by developing and using our gifts we might bless each other.

Recently a visiting teacher helped prepare a blind sister to go for the first time to the Seattle Temple. She did not assume the responsibility of the bishop, but tried to explain each part of entering the temple for one's endowment in such a way that the sightless woman could feel calm, peaceful, and spiritually in tune.

In the Doctrine and Covenants we read: "I say unto you, that as many as receive me, to them will I give power to become the sons of God, even to them that believe on my name." (D&C 11:30.)

You may think, "That can't be true! How can there be that great potential in you or me when all I see is a struggling, imperfect human being?" I can only say, as did Lorenzo Snow, "Godliness cannot be conferred but must be acquired." (Truman Madsen, *The Highest In Us* [Salt Lake City: Bookcraft, 1978], p. 9.)

You must want the Lord's blessings so much that you have faith in his word. Then you will resist worldly enticements and you will seek him in prayer. You will listen to the promptings of the Holy Spirit and proclaim his gospel within the reach of your influence. In this process you will develop your spiritual powers. "Unto as many as received me gave I power to do many miracles, . . . power to obtain eternal life." (D&C 45:8.)

Nurture your spiritual powers. It is the only way you can become what you are really meant to be.

Where do you begin to develop your physical, mental, and spiritual powers? Begin in your home. Whether you are single or married, whether your home is an apartment, a house, or a dormitory, begin in your home. Your home is the place where you go each night, but it is more than that. Your home is the place where you grow in physical stature, in mental abilities, in spiritual strengths. The scriptures clearly teach the importance of the home and the training that takes place there.

"Organize yourselves; prepare every needful thing; and establish a house, even a house of prayer, a house of fasting, a house of faith, a house of learning, a house of glory, a house of order, a house of God." (D&C 88:119.) I like to apply those words to establishing a house where gods-to-be can be taught and trained, where they can develop the habits and attitudes that will prepare them to live in a celestial home in the hereafter because they have learned how to pray and develop a sweet dependence upon the Lord, to fast and draw near unto him, to learn of him and his ways so that his purposes and work can be the direction of their lives. I feel that the phrase "prepare every needful thing" is very important. What is a needful thing? Is it a needful thing to learn how to pay rent and still have enough money for transportation and entertainment? Is it a needful thing to have good food?

Sometimes in our hurry to get everything done, fast foods have become the order of the day. We think of dinner at McDonald's— at least I'm told that they feed more people in America than any other food service except the army. I think dinner at McDonald's should be the exception rather than the rule, unless, of course, your name happens to be McDonald. I hope you will use the many resources available to you to help you supply your kitchen with good things to eat—nutritious snacks, super soups, and money-saving meals. Eating is a needful thing. It should be done with knowledge of nutritional values of food consumed.

Let me describe three homes. Let's see how these homes are organized to foster the powers within those who reside there. We'll go first to the home of Sally Peterson Brinton, a young mother who is a concert pianist. She is preparing right now to play with the Philharmonic Orchestra of her state. She has a baby-sitter caring for her three little sons while she spends these last few days in uninterrupted practice. Ordinarily she would limit her practice time at the piano to the hours when the children are in bed, but she is well aware that a flawless performance demands hours and hours of highly concentrated preparation— more than are available after the boys are asleep.

She loves music. She wants her children to love it too. Each mealtime is accompanied by classical recordings: opera, symphony, world-renowned vocalists or choirs. She is following the pattern set by her own mother. As soon as the children are old enough, they will accompany their parents to special musical events in order to firmly establish great music as an important part of their lives. I hope her example will give you a thought about how you might cultivate learning by planning for a time, a place, and a way to make possible the learning you desire.

We'll enter quietly into the next house because the fourth-grader who lives there is sobbing out the aching of the hurt he experienced today in school: "My teacher told me that I am the worst penman in the whole class!" If there is dismay at the teacher's lack of consideration for her son, the mother doesn't show it—only compassion and understanding. She carefully weighs her words, and then says, "I'm sorry. I know it hurts to have someone point out your errors and your weaknesses, but I have a thought. Why don't you practice your penmanship each day until you are the very best penman in the class?"

His tear-filled eyes begin to shine with a ray of hope. He asks, "But, how can I do it, Mother? When can I write? What will I write?"

"Every night after school you can work at the kitchen table until dinner time. Why don't you begin by copying your favorite scriptures? Or you might write words from the dictionary or even the newsworthy events from the paper. You will learn a lot. If you write very carefully and try to form each letter perfectly you will soon be a beautiful penman. It can only happen with practice. You'll have to try really hard."

That determined little boy begins. He works hard every night. By the end of the year he comes home elated. "You were right, Mother! My teacher said today, 'Theron, you are the very best penman in the class!' "

He invested the time. The place was established. He was given the encouragement. All of these are needful things, if learning is to take place.

It's Christmas Eve as we join this next family. They are at home in a strange city. It is new to them. The father has to complete his professional training, and so the whole family has had to be uprooted. At Christmas time, it is very difficult for them to be away from their extended families. They have just finished dinner as we enter the house, and so we'll follow them into the family room.

The father says: "Children, Christmas is a time of great love. Our Heavenly Father loved us, his children, enough to send his Only Begotten Son into the world on that Christmas Day so long ago. He was to be the example of righteous living. He was to teach us how to grow close to our Heavenly Father. We must live worthy of that precious gift. This Christmas Eve I would like to give you a gift that is only available to you because Jesus was born. Because of him I hold the holy priesthood of God. By that power I would like to give each of you children a father's blessing tonight. We will start with the oldest.''

One by one the children go to their father. They receive blessings suited to their special needs. Then we see each child, even the three-year old, stand and tell how he or she has been blessed by the life of Jesus. The parents then testify to their children of the abundant blessings they have received from Jesus Christ.

I believe that those children will always remember that Christmas Eve. I believe that the example set by their parents of faith and prayer will be a directional force in the lives of their children. It is a needful thing to organize and plan if such experiences are to be a part of one's life. They don't just happen.

Someone once said, ''All human power is a compound of time and patience,'' and Benjamin Disraeli said, ''All power is a trust.'' We should realize that time and patience are necessary for organizing our lives and calling forth our powers. It may begin with something as simple as bringing order to a desk, to drawers, or to the rooms where we are. We can leave each room better than when we entered it by simply picking up and by straightening it. Some people leave a trail of books, papers, clothes, boots, purses, and so forth from the front door to the bedroom if that is their destination. They either expect someone else to pick up after them or they intend to retrace their steps at another time and begin picking up their belongings. Neither of these actions is worthy of the kind of living of which I speak. It's good to believe in a future time, but it is better to surround yourself with beauties and memories born out of order today.

President J. Reuben Clark, Jr., taught that our homes are holy places and that we should approach them as if coming to an altar. Ask yourself what you have done to make your home an altar—a place that sanctifies or prepares those who are there for celestial living. Do your actions focus on developing loving relationships? Are there kindly acts of concern each day? Does your routine bring about maintenance of that home and practices of provident living? Do your pursuits bring about learning and refinement? Are the relationships within that home those that can be forever?

What is a home? To one of my friends it is a place where children are cherished and memories are born. Home is where she and her husband put the priceless antiques they collect. Home is where friends and family gather to share love. Home is a framed newspaper account of her grandmother's funeral service or an oil painting of a scene she knows and loves. Home is an attic turned into an upstairs playroom that is just filled with things meant to bring happiness to children. Home is a collection of books full of lofty thoughts that the family members make their own. Home is the kitchen where good food is prepared and gratefully enjoyed. Her home is a place where love is felt and faith and dreams are realized.

When President Ronald Reagan delivered his Inaugural Address, it was essentially based on faith in the American people. He said, "Act worthy of yourselves." He told us that we are "too great a nation to limit ourselves to small dreams."

So it is for us as Latter-day Saints. We too must act worthy of ourselves and the glorious vision of truth and eternity that has been restored to us. That vision of eternal growth and gentle, loving persuasion is too great a dream to let go when we hunger in our heart to be one with God.

The power is in you to reach out and claim those blessings.

Remember that beyond anything you have ever accomplished is the challenge of living the principles of heaven in such a way that you can connect the powers in you with the powers of heaven.

Melvin J. Ballard said: "Men came to the Savior to see what God was like; we stand to show men what Christ was like." (*Melvin J. Ballard, Crusader For Righteousness* [Salt Lake City: Bookcraft, 1966], p. 112.)

You have the powers within you to be Christlike. It's what you are meant to become.

5

Roots and Wings

I suppose there has never been a time when there has been more discussion about women more widely heard through public media, nor has there been a time when women everywhere have been more actively involved in searching for direction and in seeking to change traditional attitudes and practices concerning women. Through the power of the media, law, and government, major societal changes are now possible, and sweeping changes are being made.

Change should not be viewed with undue anxiety; it is a necessary part of the ongoing human experience. The great challenge today is to meet the ever-changing conditions with purpose and direction born of faith in God and a knowledge of his eternal principles. With this foundation, changes in our own lives and in society can be influenced to move in the direction of heaven.

In May of 1975, I attended the American Mothers Convention in New York City as a new general president of the Relief Society. Every year each state of the union selects a woman who has been an outstanding mother to represent the state at the convention.

Having stepped into a beautiful gold frame, each mother made a presentation. I will never forget one of these women. She was in the late years of her life. She spoke with love as she looked at us and quietly declared, "My children are my greatest accomplishment. My success has come, I feel, because I gave them roots and wings—roots because I helped them to have faith in the Lord Jesus Christ, and wings because I gave them faith in themselves."

I would like to take her thoughtful summation as the theme of my comments here, for in a world that is complicated, confusing, harsh at times and unacceptable at others, with the struggle for equality for women and with the many problems of personal responsibility demanding our attention, I find myself thinking that we, too, need roots and wings. One of our greatest needs is to recognize the good from the past that should be preserved and protected and to see the good from the present that should be embraced and encouraged. We need the strength of purpose that can only come from a firm foundation of faith coupled with the knowledge of the endless potential we inherit as sons and daughters of God.

One way seemed to open up when we were given approval by the First Presidency to ask the women of the Church to contribute funds to build a monument in Nauvoo as a memorial to the place where the Relief Society was organized under the direction and inspiration of the Prophet Joseph Smith. Here such a statement about faith in God and faith in self could be made. We sought earnestly for an artist's conception that would convey this important message, and we accepted the plan of Dennis Smith. As a result of his plan, thirteen sensitively sculpted figures were created—eleven by Dennis Smith and two by Florence Hansen—representing the gospel concept of woman and her relationships to the world, to be placed in a lovely garden setting. People could come to enjoy the beauty of the statues and, we hoped, to take a few moments to contemplate the truths being expressed in artistic form. There the centuries-old contributions that women have always made as individuals, wives, and mothers could be told. The magnitude of their responsibility to give birth and to nurture new life could be recognized as a contribution to be honored, not to be tossed away in the name of progress, when indeed no meaningful progress is possible without it.

The roots of faith we seek are supplied by the eternal principles of righteousness that govern both heaven and earth. The wings will come as we master ourselves, discipline our talents, and seek to become like our Father.

Consider some of the eternal truths appropriate to a discussion about a woman's destiny. As we step into that garden setting in Nauvoo, we see the central figure in the first circle of the monument—a heroic-sized statue of a woman. She represents the central, fundamental teaching of the gospel concerning women. Each woman is a unique individual, with divine potential, of infinite worth.

Some years ago when one of my daughters was a small, exuberant child, we were all sitting around the fireplace as families do at the happy Christmas season. It had been a good, satisfying, full holiday, and the stress and hustle and bustle of the day were behind us. We were enjoying the warm afterglow of this happy day. Fathers, mothers, cousins, aunts, and uncles, all chatted quietly by the fire. Into this large contented group of people who love each other bounded my child with the exclamation, "Look who's here, everybody!" Our curiosity piqued by this enthusistic announcement, we looked beyond her with interest and inquired, "Who is it?" She returned our questioning glances with sparkling eyes and a face wreathed in smiles and announced, "Me!"

It was not what we had expected, somehow, but I shall never forget that moment. This little bit of a girl taught her older kinfolk an important lesson. In a sense she was saying what the central figure represents, "There is no one more important than the individual." The individual human being is the most important entity on the face of the earth. The child of God in mortality was co-existent as an intelligence with God himself. As intelligences we knowingly chose the mortal experience with all its hazards, and once we pass the portals of death we will have the opportunity for continuing our progress eternally.

C. S. Lewis once said, "You will never meet a mere mortal. Every day you meet gods-to-be or devils-to-be and you won't know until it's an accomplished fact which is which." (*The Weight of Glory and Other Addresses* [Grand Rapids, Michigan: William B. Eerdmans Publishing Company, 1969], pp. 14-15.) That is true: The simple and magnificent message of the restored gospel is that godhood is the birthright of every child of God.

The scriptures say that God made us "a little lower than the angels" (Psalm 8:5), and that he made it possible for us to become like him by doing the things we could not do for ourselves in mortality: guaranteeing us the right of agency, and through the atoning sacrifice providing the way to salvation and exaltation.

To accomplish that noble goal, we must love the truth—love it enough to seek for it, love it enough to understand it, love it enough to live it. The truths of the gospel will make us free from doubt, from ignorance, from sin. They will give us hope for the future, faith in ourselves, strength to meet adversity, and a direction that will lead us to do much good.

I hope each woman will realize that she is a child of God sent here to act as an individual, born with all the potential of unlimited growth and achievement. One woman stated, "A woman is her Father's daughter, about her Father's business." This implies an essential and beautiful relationship between each individual woman and her creator. God values his daughters. He places an infinite value on all his children with no arbitrary inferior or superior comparative labels. He wants us to be about his business just as he wanted Jesus Christ to be, and his business is eternal, life-giving work. God's dealings with us are not capricious. He loves us too much for that. His dealings with us are predicated upon eternal principles of righteousness.

I hope every woman that looks at that central monument figure sculpted in bronze will see herself stepping forward into the future, confidently, with her head held high, knowing that there is within her the capacity for eternal progression, the strength to meet whatever situations life has to offer, and the right to choose the direction of her life.

The four supporting statues in the first circle of the monument represent four great root systems upon which a woman's life should grow if it is to have a place in the plan of the Lord. One is to develop her talents; a second, to gain knowledge and with it wisdom; a third is to learn to pray; and a fourth, to give compassionate service.

Think about the life-giving potential of each root system. The Lord has commanded us to develop our talents. Remember the parable of the talents? The Lord was well pleased with the two who doubled their talents, but he was not pleased with the one who was afraid and hid his talent, and He took it from him.

One time I was to give a lesson on talents. I talked with one of our outstanding musicians and asked him how he felt knowing that he had been given such a marvelous talent by the Lord. His reply surprised me. He said: "Most people feel a musician is automatically given that talent. I admit that a musician must have the mental capacity to comprehend and retain musical composition and that he must have hands that are whole and nimble and workable and that he must have a sensitive nature; but any musician of worth will have to work hard day after day, year in and year out, to develop his talent."

Traditionally we have acknowledged talents in the performing arts as gifts from the Lord, and they are. Those who study and write about the whole person point out that there are many other talents to be acknowledged. Gifted people in many areas have the power to enrich lives. Perhaps your developed talents will be used in volunteer work—full time, part time, or occasionally. Perhaps your talents will be needed in improving the quality of church service given in the name of the Lord. Perhaps your talents will be most useful in enriching the lives of your family—your brothers, sisters, mother, father, the husband you choose, or the children who will come into the homes you establish.

Learn to develop your talents and have experiences that will allow you to enjoy more of life's abundance, and then the enrichment in the home you create will be greater. The gospel urges us to develop every talent we have, seek the virtuous and lovely and always do those things which are of good report and praiseworthy.

The root system based on learning is a fundamental part of our faith. When the Lord placed Adam and Eve on earth he gave them two commandments: One was to multiply and replenish the earth, and the other was to subdue it. The subduing is the learning. We should learn all we can about the earth and how it functions. We should learn the laws of mortality so that we might have sufficient knowledge upon which to base our life's decisions, and thus remove ignorance from our path.

No one can know everything in mortality. That is one of the glories of the eternities. But the pursuit of knowledge, the learning little by little—one step at a time—and the setting of the mind to the ongoing excitement of learning is part of what we should do with our lives. It is an adventure. I have seen this love of learning in my doctor grandmother and in my teacher mother, and I hope I can pass it on to my children and they to theirs. When true learning takes place, we realize how much there is yet unknown and feel the thrill of accepting the challenge to pit ourselves against the unknown.

The root system concerning prayer puts us in touch with the power and light of heaven. Prayer is the means by which each human being may be in touch with heaven personally. The Lord has told us that he will send each of us knowledge to guide our lives if we will but ask. Again and again, he says, "seek, and ye shall find; knock, and it shall be opened unto you." (Matthew 7:7; see also 3 Nephi 14:7; D&C 4:7.) He is the source of the knowledge we need most, and his invitation should be accepted daily. We can no more afford to shut the door on the fine opportunities of education that exist in our day than we can afford to refuse to kneel in prayer and seek the guidance of our Heavenly Father. Both systems are essential to that quality of learning which will bring us one day into the presence of God.

Can you see why I feel it is such a glorious time to be born a woman? For centuries the world did not provide an opportunity for women to learn or use their talents or to feel that they had a significant part in the great drama of life. For many centuries ignorance darkened the world and made it difficult, if not impossible, for most of the human race to grow intellectually. The wonders of the written word were scarcely available. The truths of the scriptures were not accessible to most common people. But now they are, along with an increasing and almost overwhelming flow of knowledge. Women today are freed from many of the time-consuming household tasks of years gone by. A woman's challenge today is to choose wisely from the multitude of offerings, and to discover through prayer what blessings the Lord wishes her to claim.

The fourth root system that our bronze figures personify is compassionate service. Some of our greatest learning experiences will come as we give compassionately. We may forget to be compassionate, but God never will. It is important for us to remember that this is a significant part of our human experience. In fact, it seems to me that in all our learning, that which we obtain by way of giving compassionately is the most significant learning we ever do.

When it was time for Jesus to leave this world, in his last great sermon to his disciples he said that their eternal lives would depend upon that which they had done to alleviate suffering. (See Matthew 25:31-46.) Suffering is the great common denominator for all mortals. When we suffer we often feel that no one else suffers as we do—and yet I think back to a time when I took a little granddaughter to the hospital to have some foot braces checked. I was pained that she had to wear those heavy braces. As I waited for the doctor, many women with crippled children came to empathize and sympathize with me over her condition. Then my heart really ached, because while I knew that her correction would be full and complete soon, I could see that their children might never know full health or activity. Standing by and watching them suffer made me suffer and realize at the same time how helpless I was; but I now know of the great compassion of those women. They had developed their tender compassion for others because of problems. Perhaps this experience has made it possible for me to share more deeply in others' sorrows.

Interlacing these four root systems is another essential back-up system of roots. We might call it responsibility. Responsibility is a key word as we try to understand and relate to any idea in the world today. We have many options regarding how to spend our lives, but we must not forget that option and agency do not mean license. The fundamental concept of agency is that one who makes choices must also accept the responsibility for whatever comes of those choices.

If we are sullen in our conversation, we must accept the responsibility for such a demeanor, for it is likely that the result will be that nobody will enjoy being with us. If we waste our paychecks, the result is that we lack money for our education or supplies or food or clothing. If we do not read good books, our potential store of ideas is diminished substantially.

If we never attend cultural events, we have denied ourselves the enrichment that can come to our souls. If we have heard the gospel from our youth and never knelt to ask if it is true, we have rejected the opportunity for the motivating power of testimony in our lives. If we have heard about giving compassionate service and yet never have rendered any, we have lost the greatness of this opportunity.

If we marry and have children, we have a responsibility to those children. Some of society's most difficult problems have come because of the lack of acceptance by parents of the responsibility for their children and, in later years, by children for their parents.

The second circle of the monument in Nauvoo is designed to bring our attention to the relationships we have with others. Central to all is the relationship between the man and the woman in the marriage covenant and in the subsequent relationships that ensue in the family.

The Lord intended man and woman to be together. It is understandable, because the great creative work of exaltation requires both the man and the woman.

I understand that there are many in this life who never marry. We know that faithful sisters will be eligible for all blessings—that they will be judged, as we all will be, according to their worthiness. They will be given all they have earned, even a celestial mate if they have not found one in mortality. One of the great young single women who served on the Relief Society General Board has said, "For all we see confirms our knowledge that to be born female and a daughter of God is a privilege, wonderful, and encompassing; becoming a woman is our ultimate and creative responsibility.''

In our understanding, marriage is not merely for time; it is not for convenience; it is not for expediency. Marriage is a sacrament entered into by two people and it is designed by the Lord to be eternal in nature. It requires the best efforts of the man and the woman if it is to be a successful venture, one sufficiently sound in comradeship, in mutual support and trust, and in love to last beyond mortality.

A good marriage requires mutual agreement on major decisions. A good marriage requires that the partners give to each other the best of what both are and the best of what both may become. This kind of marriage comes not because of an infatuation; it is the kind of marriage based on love—not selfish love that is immature and purely romantic, but the selfless love described in the scriptures. With this kind of a marriage foundation, the family unit is born; and into the family come the spirit children of God, clothed in mortality by earthly parents, with every right to assume that they will have a loving place in which to grow to maturity.

Perhaps there is no greater laboratory in the world for the expression of Christlike love than exists in the family. In the close, day-to-day contact, we come to know more about giving love than we could learn in any other way. If our family situation is incomplete in this life, we have to search for those opportunities which will school our spirits in the practice of giving love. In either case, the primary responsibility of learning how to give love in its fullest, most life-giving sense lies with the individual. We must seek after those opportunities.

In the center of the second circle is the delightful sculpture of a woman playing with children. This woman could be a mother with children, or she could be a woman enjoying someone else's children—a teacher, an aunt, a friend, or anyone who shares some joyful moments of life with children and makes it possible for their beginning years to be filled with a remembrance of love. Children need loving, caring, adult companionship during those tender early years; they need to know that there are adults who care for them on a one-to-one basis. Traditionally, such love and sustenance has been provided primarily by the mother and the father. But it can be augmented by others who observe the need and have tender, willing hearts.

There is no question in my mind that the woman who gives birth to a child is by that very act assuming the responsibility for that child. Of course, in the ideal situation, both the father and the mother share in the responsibility and each fills an important need. When we have a child, we assume an awesome responsibility. We should nurture that child and give it the warmest, richest, most rewarding environment of which we are capable. Children are not an encumbrance. They should never be viewed in that light. They are a great and noble challenge. They will teach you more about yourself than you ever thought possible. They will learn from you more than you knew you were teaching.

No training we receive will be as revealing to us as our parenthood. In connection with our creative experiences, it will be the most significant training we receive for the eternities. Those who pass it by or give it to someone else will never know the power of that life-giving, life-training opportunity. There cannot be a greater work, for those who have the opportunity, than to bring forth the sons and daughters of God and teach them right principles in order that they may choose happiness and learning, not dead ends and sorrows. The second circle of this monument garden draws that sacred duty to our minds.

The challenge of being a wife and mother in today's world is great. A woman must be sure to marry the right person, in the right way, at the right time. Marriage is not an outlet nor an escape from the realities of life. Marriage is a schooling of oneself and a giving of loving service.

A beautiful young mother, a graduate of a prestigious women's college and mother of five, expressed these thoughts to me in a letter:

> The bearing and nurturing of children in a home filled with love and with the Spirit of the Lord is the great and glorious privilege of women. . . . As women we can ignore that calling by seeking

personal pleasure or power to the exclusion of homebuilding and motherhood. We can defile that calling by misusing those sacred powers of procreation. We can abort that calling by abandoning the responsibility of mothering to others. We can belittle that calling by feeling shame before the world for begetting life. We can misunderstand that calling by allowing devotion to children to exclude the development of the whole woman. We can diminish that calling by failing strenuously to engage our time and to recognize our opportunities as mothers. We can obscure that calling by becoming independent of the home and its responsibilities. One can subordinate that calling by yielding to the pressure to postpone childbearing in favor of that which could wait for later time or for eternity. We can cripple that calling by failing to prepare well for marriage and motherhood, failing to build the confidence and faith to wait (even throughout time) for a worthy companion, or failing actively and continually to build a strong marriage.

In the maturing years of a woman's life, she will find herself with new perspectives, perhaps with new opportunities, as her family responsibilities decrease. No two women will face the same problems, but as you continue to look forward to your life, know that you are capable, with the help of your Heavenly Father, of meeting all of the challenges that will come to you. If you have the roots of faith in God and the wings of faith in yourself that will carry you forth into the unknown, upward toward the eternities, they will let you soar beyond the disciplines necessary in day-to-day living.

6

Blueprints for Living

I was made very much aware of what goes into the development of a blueprint when our daughter and her husband decided to build a home. It was an exciting, new venture.

They began by looking around for a lot. When they finally found what to them was the perfect place for their house, they had it appraised and surveyed. They purchased the property. Then came hours and hours of talking and intently planning together to identify the things they both wanted in their dream home. What style should it be: French, English Tudor, colonial, a ranch-type rambler? What general floor plan should they choose; should they have one level or two? What kind of room requirements: a family room, and dining room, a kitchen, and bedrooms, of course, but how many, and where should they be located? What extras could they afford within their budget? What special needs did the family have, individually and collectively?

They began to consider how they wanted the house finished. Of what material should it be made? What colors? What type of furnishings?

They spent hours putting down on paper their ideas, needs, and wants. They sought the services of a good architect who could take their roughly sketched ideas, refine them, and then translate them into a blueprint. The blueprint had to be professionally drawn with exact detail so that it could be given to a builder who would be able to estimate the cost, materials, and the skilled craftsmen necessary to make a house from that plan.

There are so many fundamental and important decisions to make before a new home can be built. I am forcibly struck by the parallels between the process of building a home and the process of building a life.

Four similarities stand out: first, selecting your lot in life; second, building your life's foundation; third, constructing a framework for all you do; and fourth, finishing the structure by becoming what you want to be.

Let's look first at selecting the lot. Surveying the land and making choices begins early in life. As you approach adulthood you have the responsibility of assuming the control and the direction of your own life. In the decisions of adolescence you begin to look around you and form impressions of the world and the people who live in it—the people with whom you must interact. You will have certain experiences—some you choose, and others are thrust upon you by parents, peers, or circumstances.

Regardless of the circumstances, you must ultimately decide what kind of a human being you are going to be, upon what philosophies you are going to build your life, and what style of life you will live. Will your choices be based upon worldly or spiritual values? What lot will you select for your life?

What attitudes toward the experiences of mortality will you develop? Do you favor the cool, noncommittal way of breezing past events; will you assume a negative, pessimistic outlook; or will you prefer a happy, optimistic attitude?

What will you do with your life in your day-to-day living? How will you relate to the members of your family and your neighbors? Will you volunteer yourself to reach out to someone, or will you shut your eyes to everyone outside your own little circle?

What general scheme of planning will you adopt—a daily, organized routine requiring self-discipline, or will you just let things come as they may?

Where will you stand in relationship to God? Will you have a program of daily prayer and meditation, will you become a scholar of the scriptures, or will you find yourself too busy to read? Will you choose to serve the Lord or will you just wait and see what happens? What kind of time are you willing to give, and what kind of planning for a lifetime of education, training, and continual growth do you want?

Experts who study human behavior point out that there is a great need for making a lifetime plan, realistically recognizing what each period of life is likely to bring.

Alena H. Moris, president of Seattle's Individual Development Center, points out, "With some kind of a good design to life rather than a random existence which does not give security, one can lead a life that is potent and dynamic, one that provides all of the satisfaction of knowing that you are becoming what you are capable of being." (Quoted by Jean Bradshaw, *Deseret News*, April 10, 1979.)

Childhood is a special time, a time of enormous growth and development. I remember my mother once saying, "Spend all the time you possibly can with your children; they grow up so fast and leave your home that you will hardly know it is happening." I thought, "Mother, you've forgotten how long the time is when you are so hard at work with and for them." Now I know she was right. Like it or not, believe it or not, children do grow up all too quickly. In large measure, they reach out and participate in the excitement of learning only when it is encouraged and nurtured in the home and in the larger environment in which those early years are spent.

Can there be any wonder at the vital importance of the home when we realize the profound effect these early years have upon the lives of children? It is in the home where the life of a child is primarily shaped. The home is also the significant factor in determining the existence, or the nonexistence, of such basic problems in society as divorce, crime, suicide, and all manner of social disorder.

After childhood comes the period of choice and preparation, surveying the fields of interest, and focusing attention on understanding and developing personal interests and talents.

Realize your potential for study and the opportunity you have to develop new educational skills. Concentrate with single-mindedness on learning and preparing yourself with professional skills. One never gets too much education nor masters too many skills. One great principle of the gospel teaches that we need to commit ourselves to a lifetime of learning. I think that learning needs to include practical ways to apply newly acquired information.

Consciously upgrade your marketable skills, for no one knows when or where a woman might be called upon to provide the money to support herself. Elder Howard W. Hunter stated it insightfully when he said:

> There are impelling reasons for our sisters to plan toward employment also. We want them to obtain all the education and vocational training possible before marriage. If they become widowed or divorced and need to work, we want them to have dignified and rewarding employment. If a sister does not marry, she has every right to engage in a profession that allows her to magnify her talents and gifts. (*Ensign*, November 1975, p. 124.)

Select a mate with whom you can share the world's experiences and with whom you will be able to build an eternal companionship. This selection is the single most important decision one ever makes. Mortal and eternal relationships are dependent upon this choice. It will determine how you care for the children you bear, how they will increase in stature, in wisdom, and in favor with God and man.

Looking way down the road, what will happen when your children are grown and off in pursuit of their own interests? Where will you spend your time so that you can make the most of that season of your life? All of this is but a small part of that important process of selecting your lot.

Land and life are not always what they seem from the surface. A careful builder always has a contour map of the land made before his work actually begins. So should we remember in living our lives to consider the lay of the land as the Lord has counseled:

Therefore whosoever heareth these sayings of mine, and doeth them, I will liken him unto a wise man, which built his house upon a rock:

And the rain descenced, and the floods came, and the winds blew and beat upon that house; and it fell not: for it was founded upon a rock.

And every one that heareth these sayings of mine, and doeth them not, shall be likened unto a foolish man, which built his house upon the sand:

And the rains descended, and the floods came, and the winds blew, and beat upon that house; and it fell: and great was the fall of it. (Matthew 7:24-27.)

No structure can long stand upon land that is faulty. Sandy soil will wash away, and no matter how strong the structure upon it, that building will be destroyed. So it is with all people. Those who choose to live in shaky, immoral environments will have to recognize that the nature of the soil upon which they build will bring about their destruction.

The second phase of constructing a home or a life is building a firm foundation. Revelation from the Lord is the great foundation stone of all happy, productive living. He is the source of all truth and reliable knowledge. He extends an open invitation to come to him for information, for direction, and for rest in times of trials and tribulations.

The Lord invites you to seek a personal testimony of truth concerning the existence of eternal things as the fundamental strength of your life. Time and time again we find the words in the scriptures, "knock and it shall be opened unto you." In fact, the Topical Guide to the Scriptures tells us this invitation appears thirteen times in the Bible, the Book of Mormon, and the Doctrine and Covenants. This seems to be a very important detail in a blueprint for living. It is repeated often—carefully, simply, and compellingly: "Behold, I stand at the door, and knock: if any man hear my voice, and open the door, I will come in to him, and will sup with him, and he with me." (Revelation 3:20.)

The fundamental unity of Latter-day Saint women comes from the one thing that each of us can have by our own diligent effort: a testimony of the plan of life and salvation and the witness that

God lives. This testimony gives us the knowledge that we are his children and that we individually have access to the powers of heaven.

The journals of the early Mormon women of this dispensation tell us that before finding the gospel they were seeking light and truth, and they could not find satisfaction in their souls that what they had was enough. Then they heard about Joseph Smith, or they heard about the golden plates, or the elders came knocking at their doors and told them the truth had been restored. They asked the Lord if what they were hearing was true, and the light came into their lives. They wrote that the witness of the Holy Spirit was like a light being turned on in their souls. They would not and could not be persuaded otherwise.

Sister Eliza R. Snow says that her father, in assisting widows and others, was detained until the very last day of grace allotted to the Mormons for leaving the county; the weather was very cold, indeed, and the ground was covered with snow. She walked on to warm her aching feet until the teams would overtake her. Meanwhile she met one of the so-called militia. The man roughly and abruptly accosted her with the harsh words, "This will cure you of your faith!" The young heroine looked him steadily in the eye and replied, "It will take more than this to cure me of my faith." His countenance fell and he responded, "I must confess you are a better soldier than I am." ("Eliza R. Snow, As Seen Through the *Woman's Exponent,* 1872-1887," unpublished manuscript compiled and edited by Shirley Anderson Cazier.)

Those early women of Mormondom had a personal witness that the gospel was restored and that they could become part of building the kingdom of God on earth. In this great work they would be part of taking that glad message of testimony throughout the world. I suppose the poet captured the feelings of their quest and the personal nature of this spiritual foundation in their lives when he declared:

> Back into the heart's small house I crept,
> And fell upon my knees and wept.
> And lo! He came to me.
> (Authorship Unknown.)

The strongest, firmest, most sure foundation for life is a personal testimony of the truth that God lives, that he speaks again to us, and that he cares for each of us. This testimony will come to you if you will ask in faith, nothing wavering, and with sincere intent. Thousands of Latter-day Saint women have a testimony of the gospel of Jesus Christ today, and it can be yours, too, if you will but ask the Lord in constant, secret prayer.

Third, any good house blueprint calls for a strong framework upon which to build. So it is with life. Each individual needs to construct a strong framework upon which to build. In building a house one selects good, firm timbers or strong, tempered steel that can bear the weight of the rest of the structure and withstand the ravages of storm and disaster.

In building a life, a person needs to choose good, strong tenets and assemble them into a design that gives stability and unity and yet allows for the constant addition of new information and further insights. This is the essence of gospel teaching.

The blueprint from the Lord makes clear the need to build our lives on a personal quest for eternal perfection. It is achieved line upon line, precept upon precept; each new insight will give greater vision. When one seeks to be constantly improving, overcoming faults and weaknesses and searching for enriching, enlarging opportunities, life becomes full of meaningful experiences.

Remember, though, that perfection is a process, not a state achieved. You are continually involved in learning today what will give you the information and the experience you need for tomorrow.

We should give service and perform acts of compassionate care to others throughout our lives. Doing this allows us to develop godlike attributes.

Holding the framework securely together, and essential to every addition, is charity. Without charity all else is as "sounding brass, or a tinkling cymbal" (1 Corinthians 13:1).

Charity is the pure love of Christ—everlasting love—and except we have charity we cannot be saved. Further, we are shown in the Lord's blueprint that we should have charity for all, even those who despitefully use us, and that without charity all we do is of no value.

If you choose this sound, basic structure, you will have a life with endless potential. You will be able to spend your lifetime finishing the structure—completing it, furnishing it, enriching it. That is why it is important to have a good blueprint. You can make your plans with such care that the structure will stand firm and unshakable. You can then imaginatively and creatively go forward with the finishing work of your house.

You can set in priority the items you want and then one by one add to your life until that structure is complete. In your day-to-day living, that means beginning to develop within yourself the attributes that make you the kind of person you want to be.

When you begin may not be nearly so important as that you do begin. The gospel provides a vision of your fulfillment as a woman, an understanding of your future as an eternally oriented human being—a woman who is strong, competent, and filled with capabilities and commitment to a quest that will keep you constantly achieving.

You feel grateful that you need not be fearful of life, for the Savior came to show the way and to conquer death. His atonement made possible your salvation and even exaltation.

So if you are willing to accept the gospel blueprint and adapt the framework design to your own life, you can move forward, encouraged to finish your unique structure by developing all of your talents. You will look to the future with enthusiasm, for the Lord has removed the hopelessness of death and has taught that even errors are to be viewed as learning experiences.

Nothing that is for your good is forbidden. Cautionary signs warn of those things that bring sorrow and unhappiness. Fundamentally, this mortal experience is to give you a variety of situations in which you can test yourself and develop the qualities that will make you worthy to return again and dwell with him who made you.

When builders are working on a new structure, and the threat of bad weather comes or winter approaches, they quickly proceed to enclose the structure. I've heard at least two reasons for this. First, good builders want to get the outer shell completed so that they can work throughout the storms to complete the inside of the building; second, they want to protect the interior from the ravages of bad weather because usually the materials used in finishing the structure are not designed to withstand the elements in the same way as those on the outside. Lives are like that, too. Early commitment to eternal truth allows the closure of the framework, and gives us the protection we need to withstand the ravages of society's ills. It also provides a shield to protect us during the perfecting of our souls.

I do not offer these suggestions as a matter of preferential priority, but I do suggest that both exterior and interior finish work are necessary. In fact, the finishing work in building a life is never completed. It goes on throughout mortality and throughout eternity. Change from the outside will occur just as surely as the sun rises and sets. Change from the inside will occur also, but improvements only come when we make them happen. If we just drift, the internal changes will be for the worse. If we determine to work to achieve goals we can have personal, internal growth, gracious and beautiful, worthy of our eternal potential.

Transferring your general ideas onto a blueprint and then transforming the drawings into reality requires completing many carefully detailed tasks and making countless thoughtful decisions. This is the fourth element in building your life—finishing the structure. It is the work of a lifetime.

In looking to the exterior finishing, be aware of the great variety of exteriors available. No two women look exactly alike. It was never the intent of the Lord that they should. He enjoins you to know and understand the workings of your body and thereby comprehend what helps and what hurts its functions.

A healthy body is more pleasing to look at and its movement more graceful, thus affording the benefits of both looking and feeling better. One Relief Society general board member strives for a physically fit body by jogging in her room and memorizing scriptures at the same time—surely a pleasing combination.

The adornment of the human body is another point of exterior finish. It involves what we wear, our makeup, jewelry, grooming habits, style preferences.

Brigham Young told the people there was reason to believe that the angels of heaven were lovely to look upon. He encouraged the sisters to be neat and clean and beautiful. He also felt strongly that fashion excesses were to be avoided. I think the balance should still concern us.

We should keep ourselves neat and clean. Some time spent in making ourselves attractive is important as it makes us feel better and other people feel better about us.

There is wisdom in developing one's sense of style. I once knew a young, attractive buyer in a large department store. She gave a talk to some blind women, at their request, about fashion and style. They had invited her to come to a meeting they hold regularly for the purpose of helping them improve their looks.

She sat in that room as the preliminaries were being handled and looked at these well-dressed, sightless women. I don't know what thoughts went through her mind, for she was a woman trained and sensitive to the visual line and color of ready-made dresses and coats.

But when she stood up and talked, she explained to them the one thing that was the most useful for them to know. I have thought about this many times since, and I believe it is the single most useful thing for any of us to know about clothes.

"Fashion," she said, "has to do with fad and style. That which is high fashion is often faddish in nature. It will be good for a short season, and then it will be gone. Style, on the other hand, is the fashion line which is classic in nature. It will always be in good taste, with perhaps minor alterations now and then."

It is important to be mindful of the cautions given in the past that we not become slaves to appearance and that we not put undue emphasis on externals. Nevertheless, how we look is important. Costume designers for dramatic productions spend their lives studying and understanding the language of external human appearances. These appearances become very clever. They can create a mood; they can tell about a person's experiences in life; they can even tell about a person's attitude toward life.

Sometimes on the stage, as in life, a costume will give a complete insight into a person's character and feeling. A very dramatic example of this occurs in the play *The Prime of Miss Jean Brodie*. Miss Brodie is a flamboyant teacher of young girls who has dedicated her life to molding and shaping the minds and characters of her charges. She is very romantic and somewhat unrealistic. The colors and the fabrics used for Miss Brodie's costume visually portray these facets of her character in the scene where she comes into conflict with the headmistress. At the moment she is dismissed from her position, she pulls on a gray coat; as the top button is buttoned, the gray covers all the vibrant romantic color, and we see the transformation of Miss Brodie. The color and the line of the coat subtly reinforce the pathos of the play.

The clothes we wear and the appearance we choose to create have a major impact upon the course of our lives. We all respond to the visual appearance of people, and to our own appearance. We must make personal decisions about our exterior finish.

Another aspect of this exterior finish is the matter of manners —social behavior patterns, attitudes, and the effect they have upon our relationships with others.

I would not like to leave you with the feeling that appearances and external relationships are so important as to justify spending all of our time with them. They are not, and we must use restraint and good judgment so that we do not waste precious time or become vain. But our exterior finish does influence our life. It invites people to you and to some extent governs their attitudes toward you. It is also true that what you wear, and how you look, and how you think about yourself influences how you feel.

In the film *West Side Story*, Maria first discovers her feelings of loving and she sings, "I feel pretty, oh so pretty . . ." Of course, it is proverbial that a woman in love looks beautiful.

A stage designer I know once conducted a workshop for the Church. As he was teaching the volunteers how to make costumes, some wanted to use a shortcut and hem the period skirts by machine. Painstakingly he explained that the hand-stitched hems looked better because they would flow and move more easily. "That's important on the stage," he said, "because it helps the actress. If she feels that she looks graceful, she will perform better."

This is the reason I mention outward appearances and manners. They are necessary to complete your life. The exterior finish of the house is what invites us in.

But of far greater significance is the finish on the inside. On the inside lies true beauty. On the inside lies the motivation for all that we do. You can select and polish those characteristics for which you wish to be known. Will you be honest? Will you be chaste? Will you be kind? Will you have integrity?

You and I alone determine the interior finish of our own souls. The choices we make individually are the ones that ultimately set in place the furnishings.

Will you be part of the creative force that allows human life to continue on this earth? Only your personal decisions concerning the bearing of children, if you have a choice, can determine that. Will you be part of the rearing of children? Only your decisions and actions can determine that.

Will you marry if a mutually satisfying opportunity comes your way? Only you can decide that.

Will you be lonely in this life? Probably. Everybody knows some loneliness. But will your loneliness engulf you and stop your progress? Only you can decide that. Single or married, you will have times of choice in your life. Will you seek out opportunities to give love, or won't you? Only you can decide, but upon that decision so much else depends. One thing is certain: If you give love to all you encounter—and if you seek opportunities to give love to those who hunger and thirst and have great need—then love will flow back to you, and you will not be alone.

So it goes, down the whole catalogue of human characteristics. Which ones do you wish to have? Which ones are you willing to cultivate and develop? The interior finish of your life depends upon such decisions.

One of the great teachings of the restored gospel is that each person has the right and the responsibility to determine the direction of his or her life. So it is with you. So it is with me.

The English writer Somerset Maugham, who is known as a great cynic, once wrote a book called *Summing Up*. In this volume he describes each of the Christian virtues and puts them down one by one as being full of fraud or hypocrisy. Then he comes toward the end of the book, and he writes that, despite his disillusionment with these so-called virtues, when he finds himself in the presence of a truly good person his heart kneels in reverence.

So finish your interior with the characteristics of faith, hope, and charity, remembering that the greatest of these is charity. Seek wisdom and give service freely. In these ways you will adorn your life with the beauties that radiate from within.

Circumstances and opportunities will vary for each of us. You have to seek out those opportunities which will allow you to develop, and you must be responsible for the choices you make as well as the consequences of those choices for yourself, for others, and for the society in general.

The Lord requires only that you do the best you can to gain experience and that you continue your growth by participating with a teachable spirit and a willing heart.

7

Prepare Ye! Prepare Ye!

In a sacrament meeting in Hawaii a young speaker told of his experiences on a three-day hike. The first day, just three hours onto the trail, he realized that his shoes weren't right for the trip. The rocks were jagged and piercing. His loafers weren't sturdy enough. One shoe caught on a sharp rock and the heel fell off. There was no time to try to stick it back on so he just kept going, even though he limped a little with one foot flatter than the other. That didn't matter too much, though, because before long the other heel was snagged off too.

The second day he was making it pretty well with his two flat shoes when a strap pulled loose on his pack and his sleeping bag rolled into a muddy hole. He was beginning to know why they had all been told to check out their equipment. Although it was oozing mud, he was able to tie the sleeping bag back on well enough to get to camp. That evening his Scoutmaster helped him fix the pack.

By the third day, after a night in a soggy sleeping bag, he was convinced that he had not been prepared for the trip. He should have listened to his mother. In his boyish exuberance and impatient zeal he hadn't done the things that she had suggested and that would have made his pack trip more nearly meet his expectations. But he did realize it. As you might guess, the subject of his sacrament meeting talk was preparation. He had learned—painfully—its meaning.

Have in mind that as you journey through life, you too are preparing. Then see to it that what you are learning does not stop with you but is taught again to others, perhaps around your family dinner table, with your car pool or lunch group, or with a shut-in you visit. You will learn more and you will remember it longer. You will want to remember because it is, for you, long-range preparation for that which is to come.

I know of one family in which every child was required to bring a newly learned idea to the dinner table each evening. It couldn't be something dredged up from an earlier time or left over from yesterday. It had to be discovered that very day. Often it came from scripture reading, so it wasn't new in the sense of having just been written or invented, but new to the person who understood it for the first time or didn't realize before that it was there. At other times it was the new thinking of a great philosopher, scientist, mathematician, or perhaps a newly created work of art. Their discussions were lively, punctuated by questions from the father who often played the part of the learner to improve the child's grasp of his subject.

I had the benefit of those discussions when years later a daughter of that family taught the Social Relations lessons in our Relief Society. I was a young mother at the time and particularly appreciative of the wisdom and the breadth of knowledge she evidenced in the lessons she taught. The ideas she expressed were wonderfully expansive because she had so much information from which to draw.

You do not know when, at some later time, the teachings of another time will have value to you; but you can be fairly confident that the reservoir of truth you are building and retaining will find its use.

The parable of the ten virgins provides us with a telling example of the worth of preparation and the meaning of a ready reservoir. As the ten kept their watch, five filled their lamps, five did not. We really do not know why they did not, but what we do learn from this story is that there are some things that can only be ours through personal preparation.

Our gospel experience verifies this truth. We can share the light of the gospel as one can share the glow of a lamp. But the oil, that which causes the light to burn, can only come from within, from deep reservoirs of faith and testimony filled by learning and living the truths of the gospel.

Donna Greenwood was one who had her lamp trimmed and burning when she was called to meet the Savior. I was a ward Relief Society president when, at our request, Sister Greenwood was called to be a teacher in Relief Society. My counselors and I met with her about serving as the Visiting Teaching message leader. Although she was willing to do this, we learned through our conversation with her that she had always longed to be a Spiritual Living teacher. When we asked if she would like to serve in that position, she was delighted. She said that she really didn't think she was ready for it but if she could have that privilege she would study hard and she would fast and pray for the direction of the Holy Spirit.

For the next few years Sister Greenwood was our Spiritual Living teacher. I recall her first lesson and how she trembled as she bore her testimony. She did work very hard and, through her intense faith, became a fine teacher. When, in her last year, she learned that she had terminal cancer, she found also that she had a great reservoir of strength that enabled her to meet this final test. Through her hours of study and preparation, her learning and teaching, she had gained a store of truth, and a deep testimony from which she could draw in that critical time. During all those years Sister Greenwood was preparing to teach her lessons, she always taught them first to her family.

Difficult as it was for her to think of leaving her dear husband and family of young children, she had solace in knowing that she had taught them the truths of the gospel, and she faced death with faith and fortitude. Her husband was consoled because of the eternal commitments they shared and the children had a lasting memory of the teachings of their mother to light their way in the years to come.

The reservoirs of the virgins' lamps were security against darkness of night. Our faith and testimony are a protection against darkness of spirit.

There are other kinds of reservoirs well known in desert lands. They store water against a time of need and make it possible to live in arid climates. We don't always know when there will be a dry season, but they come. With adequate preparation we can weather such times. We can store sufficient life-giving water to get us through. We may all experience an arid place. There may come dry seasons and difficult times that we can survive because of our preparation.

Learning itself is valuable preparation. The admonition of the Lord in section 93 of the Doctrine and Covenants to "obtain a knowledge of history, and of countries, and of kingdoms, of laws of God and man," helps us realize the importance of secular as well as sacred learning as the "will" of the Lord for us (D&C 93:53).

The president of Barnard College, Rosemary Park, when talking about the worth of an education for women, stated her belief that a woman's learning may prove to be most valuable when she reaches age sixty. She suggested that it is not during the more active years that knowledge is of most value to a woman—it is when she is less busy and may have fewer immediate demands that her mind's store will prove to be her richest resource. One example is a woman I know whose education enabled her first to teach school, then to provide creative learning activities for her growing children, and then for her grandchildren in her maturing years. But as she grew older and the children were no longer near, she continued to find many new interests. Now eighty-three, she and her husband have recently enrolled in a computer class at the local community college. Evenings find them enthusiastically studying their new computer language, appropriately called BASIC.

Henry Wadsworth Longfellow, when asked how he kept his agility of mind, pointed to a gnarled apple tree near his study window and replied: "I take a lesson from that tree. Every year I continue to study enough to produce sufficient new wood to put forth fresh blossoms. Without this new wood there could be no

blossoms. But with it, the blossoms on that old tree are as frag-
rant as those on the young stripling across the lawn.''

I believe that education for women is often misunderstood.
Although a young woman may appropriately engage in career-
oriented learning during her years of preparation, it is unfortu-
nate for her if, as a young mother, she thinks that the only good
use of that knowledge is in the workplace.

I appreciate this statement by Norman Corwin:

> In an important sense the home is a miniscule world. If it has ten
> books, it is partly a library: If three pictures, a little museum: If six
> tools, a repair shop: . . . Whenever a piano or fiddle is in serious
> use, it is a part-time conservatory. At mealtime grace, or in answer-
> ing a child's questions about God, it is a fraction of a church. In
> sickness, it is a hospital: . . . A screen and projector make it a
> collapsible movie house.
>
> One child makes a home a course in liberal education for both
> himself and parents: Two children make it a private school: Three or
> more make it a campus.

A woman with a fine education who also has small children at
home may want to remember that according to our faith we are
preparing to create worlds of our own. Every bit of knowledge she
can bring to bear in her home will not be too much.

Just as some women believe that career-oriented learning requires mothers to work out of the home, some other women do
not want to learn anything about mothering because they do not
have children.

I believe mothering to be one of the most important things a
woman can learn in mortality. A young, attractive friend has
quite a glamorous job working in the television industry. She
heard me make that statement one day and later said that it has
given her cause for serious reflection, even active concern.
Because she has no children, she has begun looking about for
ways that she can learn the attitudes and skills of mothering.

As a grandmother I am now looking to find new ways that I
can continue to use the skills I learned as a mother and add to
them from this perspective. What can I give to my children and to
their children that will help them find more joy in their lives and
provide better direction and greater safety in a world of increasing

immorality, violence, and crime? The skills acquired by all conscientious mothers—those whose children are with them, grandmothers, and those who are simply learning mothering ways—will provide great growth, endless usefulness, and eternal significance.

Preparation assists us in using vocational or career training to enrich a home, and it is essential to those who work outside the home, those who must work, men and women. Fulfillment in life is difficult without competence, and competence depends upon preparation. But should we desire to be not just competent, but extraordinary, this will require inordinate preparation.

In March of 1982 the women's organizations of the Church held a series of concerts in some of the major cities of the United States. Highly recognized Latter-day Saint women artists were invited to perform—those who had excelled, who were at the very peak of their careers. Before curtain time I went backstage to greet these brilliant performers, only to find them still preparing although there had been countless hours, endless days and weeks and months, and even years of practice before this night.

They were exercising their fingers, if they were pianists, and then wearing heavy gloves or holding hot potatoes wrapped in aluminum foil to keep their fingers limber. One beautiful dancer was warming up in heavy sweat pants. The vocalists were singing scales. Instrumentalists were tuning up. Preparation was continuing to be made right up until they stepped on stage. I came to understand that a flawless performance is no happenstance; it must be earned.

To be outstanding, you will need to know not just enough to get by, but everything you can learn in your field. This may include a large amount of highly specialized information that will rarely be used but that may make the difference when it is needed.

There is a way to help you do this. It is simple but encompassing. As Henry James stated, "Be the kind of a person on whom nothing is lost."

My grandmother became a successful physician by being such a person. She attended Brigham Young Academy and was in the first class that was graduated. That was in the days of Karl G.

Maeser, and he so impressed upon his students the importance of learning and not wasting their time in frivolity that when my grandmother taught school, she found additional work in a physician's office. Being a person on whom nothing was lost, she learned the practice of medicine from observing the doctor. She was such an earnest and able student that he often instructed her as he cared for his patients.

Teaching school and working in the doctor's office were merely interim steps to prepare her for medical school. There she lost no opportunity to add to her skills and was able to earn degrees in medicine, surgery, and, surprisingly, in electricity.

To the person alert to take advantage of every opportunity, nothing is lost. Every situation is potentially a chance to learn something. One article I noted recently described a man standing in a check-out line at a garden supply store. He took this opportunity to learn from the people around him. By the time he reached the cash register he had learned all about mealy bugs and their extermination, the sprinklers most successfully used on large lawns, and the pros and cons of certain insecticides. He pointed out that although all of that information might not be useful to him, some of it might, and he was there no longer than if he had learned nothing.

One high school student was successful in part-time and summer employment because, as he said, he prepared himself to be indispensable to his employer by not only learning his job, but observing and practicing until he could do any of the jobs in the business if called upon. He was not overly aggressive but was willing, honest, and anxious to help. Although working in that business was not a permanent vocation for him, the skills he developed there have been a reservoir of strength that has proved continually useful. By serving superbly in one job he was preparing in ways he had not realized for later vocational needs. Skills truly mastered are rarely lost.

Vocational or professional preparation is usually defined by minimum requirements, but the extraordinary person will continue to prepare. The finest teacher will not rely on the same notes every year, but each class will be exciting because of the new insights and information the teacher has this time that he or she did not have last time.

Maybe we can understand these instances where individuals have grasped every opportunity to increase their proficiency in their work, but how many of us have prepared to take advantage of a time when we do not have work? We might give thought to what we would do to make a dry season prove profitable. One woman wrote to me of the plight of her family when her husband lost his job.

> As the weeks went on we found it was difficult to keep our spirits on an even keel. Because people in a stressful situation waste much physical energy on worry, it was difficult to attend to normal daily duties or have enough patience with each other. That is when we had to take time to go on a walk, take the children to the park, or do something as a break from the worry.
>
> I thought with my husband around the house more, we would get a lot of odd jobs done that had been piling up. I soon found that he didn't have the heart to tackle them and it was best not to add any more pressure to the burden he was already carrying.

She continues to tell how they finally met the challenge of this difficult circumstance. Once again, it was by accepting every possible way to improve their situation. In each of these examples there is that sure element of preparation, of being the kind of a person on whom nothing is lost.

Sometimes the results of our efforts to prepare can only be seen clearly with reflection. For example, a policeman I know lost his job when the police force was cut back. He had wanted very much to be a policeman and had worked hard to get his training. While putting himself through school he had worked as a butcher to pay for his education. That preparation was such that he could reach back and use that old skill of butchering to support his family's needs in the current emergency.

What difference will your preparation make now, in twenty years, or in five? Will you have skills to see you through times of change or stress?

Your experience can help you have insight. It can help you recognize the truths that give direction and strength, truths that prompt a desire in you to go forth prepared to use your knowledge. Whatever areas of interest and preparation you pursue, there is one area that should be the focus of all you do—your home. The place where you reside, whether alone or with others, deserves your attention.

I have listened to the prophets and the apostles and I believe they are telling us that our home exerts the major influence upon our attitude toward life. Whether we spend most of our time there, or but a few waking hours, its impress will be deeply felt.

If, therefore, there are things we wish to change or overcome, we should look first to our homes and there establish some expression or manifestation of our ideal. The familiar "Charity begins at home" remains in use not because it is old but because it is true. A person learns to be charitable first at home. The elements of that Christlike love—kindness, long-suffering, rejoicing in truth, humility, and patience—are the very qualities that should characterize the atmosphere of the place where we live.

Could we look at the earthly home of Jesus of Nazareth, we would ascertain what made it a fit abode to nurture the Son of God, the Savior of mankind. Let us try to determine what might have taken place there to prepare him to go forth and preach to all the world.

There was Joseph, a father to Jesus during his years in that earthly home. We see him first as the bridegroom who believed in the angel's message concerning Mary. It was his faith and obedience, too, that later led him to take Mary and the baby to Egypt for safety. This man of faith was Jesus' mentor in the carpenter's shop where, as a young man, he no doubt learned of the devotion of a disciple along with the discipline of his trade.

Let us look at one more reference to Jesus' early training, the last mention before his ministry began. I am particularly moved by this account of his mother, Mary, asking him to turn the water to wine because it reveals to us some of what she had pondered so long in her heart. She knew who he was and what he could do. She didn't say to him, "see if you can change that vat of water to wine." She simply stated, "They have no wine." In reading the account we wonder whether perhaps he needed his mother to express her faith in him, for she directed the servants, "Whatsoever he saith unto you, do it." We don't really know how he would have demonstrated his sonship had it been otherwise. But what we do know is that he did perform his first recorded miracle at his mother's urging and with the security of her confidence in him.

We can wonder, too, where he learned the compassion that would not allow him to send the five thousand home hungry. What had happened earlier to move him to heal the lame and the leprous who flocked to him? While we know his training was unusual, we believe that he knew love in his home, for we read of his mother's anxious inquiry when he was missing for three days and again of her sorrowing at the foot of the cross.

If we would emulate the home life of the Savior, we should prepare a place where each family member would learn the discipline of obedience, faith in our Heavenly Father, and love for others as children of God.

Can we think of our homes as training places for each one to go forth and take his word near or far? For over twenty years we have been hearing that every member should be a missionary. What have we done in our homes to cause this to come about, to develop disciples of Jesus Christ, to declare the good news of the gospel to all the world? Can you envision the strength and confidence with which a young man or woman would enter the Missionary Training Center if, in fact, his home had been a missionary training center? Can you think of the work a missionary would be ready to do if the early preparations had been made, if already he or she had practiced living the ways of the Lord at home?

After a birthday dinner for one of our four daughters, I went to the kitchen to clean up. Immediately after me came a little three-year-old granddaughter. She pulled the footstool up to my side and said, "I want to help you do the dishes." I was pleased to have her there and she did a fairly good job for such a little girl. Her training was obvious. But the thing that delighted me most was that as she worked she began singing softly, "Where love is, there God is also." What a marvelous thing it will be if she is taught to continue that habit of being anxious to do the routine household chores, and then in that same sweet spirit of gladness to sing praises to our Father as she does them.

Think of the growth of the Church through the missionary effort if not one third but virtually every young man was preparing for a mission and every young woman making ready to spend her life in sharing the gospel, whether as a full-time missionary or as a neighbor, friend, or associate. The poignant scene of almost every Thursday morning at the Missionary Training Center would be expanded. We would see more and more families bringing their sons and daughters there and bidding them a tender farewell as they embark on their dedicated service.

Imagine the great growth that would come not only to the Church but to the individuals who are learning how to walk in the Savior's footsteps. Consider the impact of Section 109 of the Doctrine and Covenants if that beautiful prayer blessed each member of the household:

> We ask thee, Holy Father, that thy servants may go forth from this house armed with thy power, and that thy name may be upon them, and thy glory be round about them, and thine angels have charge over them;
>
> And from this place they may bear exceedingly great and glorious tidings, in truth, unto the ends of the earth, that they may know that this is thy work, and that thou has put forth thy hand, to fulfil that which thou hast spoken by the mouths of the prophets, concerning the last days. (D&C 109:22-23.)

The Lord has placed glorious opportunities here for each of us.

If you thirst for knowledge you will never be satiated. The thirst for knowledge motivates you to spend your lifetime adding to your reservoirs of wisdom and learning. Then out of the depth of your understanding you may partake of all of the enriching, ennobling promises that can be now and in worlds yet to come because you have followed that counsel, "Prepare ye! Prepare ye!"

8

Neither Is the Woman Without the Man

The room seemed bigger than any room could possibly be. The shadows in the recesses of the ceiling appeared dark, even forbidding. The water looked cold and deep. Everyone was dressed in white. Each face was grave. It had all been explained, and Sharon had been happy about the prospect. Now, everything was frightening. She trembled, and then, he walked toward her, hand outstretched, love in his eyes, and reassurance in his voice. She laid her shaking hand trustingly in his. As they descended into the water together all fear vanished. The steady step, the firm grip, the strong, reverent voice made the baptism beautiful and unforgettable. This beloved person who held the power of the priesthood was helping her to enter into God's church, comforting and sustaining her.

Again there came a moment of fright mingled with awe when as a small girl she sat on a chair before a sea of faces—all smiling but suddenly all strange. Then her beloved father placed his hands on her head, followed by those of others she knew and loved. "Receive the Holy Ghost." These good men, these friends, this father—through the power of the priesthood they were giving to her another gift of God.

The years passed. Sharon awoke in the middle of the night with a terrible pain, with fever, and fear. Her cry in the night was quickly answered by anxious parents. It was storming and the country doctor could not be reached. She grew worse. Dimly in her pain, she heard her father's voice, "The Lord will bless her." She felt again the beloved hands ministering to her, the calm voice of faith calling upon a loving Heavenly Father for help. The answer came in deep sleep and restored health.

These remembered and treasured moments were strung together on a long cord of memory that included incidents of bishops and dedicated leaders all doing things for her. And yet she wasn't satisfied. She had grown up in a democracy. People were to be equal. Was she equal to her brother who held this marvelous power that had blessed her throughout her life but that she could not hold? Was she living in the twentieth century or was she living in the past when women were considered inferior and incapable of doing great things? Why should women be treated differently from men? They could preside over her. She never could preside over them. Was it fair?

Sharon became a bit militant, rebellious, and jealous. She went away to college. One afternoon a group of her university friends were gathered together. Among them was a recent divorcée. All had been questioning her for an hour about her faith. One of the group said, "I know that there are other Christian churches that do not let women hold priestly offices, but still I can't understand how you or any modern American woman of the twentieth century can belong to a modern faith that discriminates against women by not letting them hold the priesthood. Your women are not equal to men. It's a return to the Dark Ages."

Before Sharon could reply, the non-Mormon divorcée spoke up: "I can understand how. I've just lived through several bitter years while my marriage fell to pieces. If I had felt that my husband had the authority to act in God's name, I might have treated him with greater respect. I might have helped him more. I might have been more understanding. Instead I competed with him. If I had held the priesthood, too, it would have been just like it was. Both of us trying to 'rule' the household—each trying to be head.

"Now that I'm feeling less bitter as time goes by, and I have long, lonely nights in which to think, I ask, 'Does it matter who is head?' Someone has to be the chairman. If we had had children, I would have been so occupied in caring for them, I would have welcomed his assuming the lead."

In these last days when militant voices fill the land, it is necessary to keep a spiritual balance, for the Lord has warned us that in this time men and women "seek not the Lord to establish his righteousness, but every man walketh in his own way" (D&C 1:16).

Do we walk in our own way, or do we try to understand and live according to our Lord's pattern? Do we trust him? Are we keeping in mind the blessings?

Let's go back to Sharon. After Sharon graduated from the university, she married. This time she was again dressed in white and surrounded by those she loved, but there was no fear as the simple, inspiring, beautiful words were spoken. The vows were taken that would bind Sharon to her beloved husband forever, the power of the priesthood sealing and promising such great blessings.

In time Sharon had a baby. Her whole world changed. Who protected her, cared for her, loved her in her hours and days of need? Again, man, in the sustaining, reassuring role of husband and father. She grew thoughtful and began to search the scriptures.

"Nevertheless neither is the man without the woman, neither the woman without the man, in the Lord." (1 Corinthians 11:11.) "And the Gods said: Let us make an help meet for the man, for it is not good that the man should be alone." (Abraham 5:14.)

She read in the Doctrine and Covenants: "Then shall they be gods, because they have no end; therefore shall they be from everlasting to everlasting, because they continue; then shall they be above all, because all things are subject unto them. Then shall they be gods, because they have all power, and the angels are subject unto them." (D&C 132:20.)

She noted that the word *they*, not *he*, was used. As a unit they could be exalted. Singly, it was not possible.

Gradually Sharon began to understand the great, grand unity

of a man and woman who are husband and wife. She read the
words of the Elder John A. Widtsoe of the Council of the Twelve:

> In the Church there is full equality between man and woman.
> . . . This doctrine of equality is confirmed in the ordinances of the
> Church, which are alike for man and woman. . . . The rewards, such
> as the gift of the Holy Ghost, and the temple ordinances, are alike.
> . . . Only those who are united, as husband and wife, by the sealing
> power, can attain exaltation in the celestial glory in the hereafter.
> . . . And provision will be made for the righteous who live unmarried
> to receive the sealing blessing in the hereafter, through vicarious
> work performed in our temples. (*Evidences and Reconciliations,* 1st ed.
> [Salt Lake City: Bookcraft, 1943], p. 241.)

Within this pattern of unity in the beginning of mankind, a
division of labor was set forth. Woman was given the privilege of
bearing the children and being their mother. Man as the father
was designated to be the provider and head of the household.
Each role is an honored and respected one because it is a divinely
given role. Each man and woman in carrying out his or her role
blesses the other. In addition, Elder Widtsoe wrote:

> No man who understands the gospel believes that he is greater than
> his wife, or more beloved of the Lord, because he holds the Priest-
> hood, but rather that he is under the responsibility of speaking and
> acting for the family in official matters. It is a protection to the
> woman who, because of her motherhood, is under a large physical
> and spiritual obligation. Motherhood is an eternal part of Priest-
> hood. It is a wise provision that the man, who is the freer to move
> about both at home and abroad, should be called to the family presi-
> dency and be under the responsibility of holding the Priesthood.
> This does not limit equality among men and women. (*Evidences and
> Reconciliations,* pp. 244-45.)

Sharon found the counsel of the Prophet Joseph Smith:

> Sisters . . . treat them [husbands] with mildness and affection. When
> a man is borne down with trouble, when he is perplexed with care
> and difficulty, if he can meet a smile instead of an argument or a
> murmur—if he can meet with mildness, it will calm down his soul
> and soothe his feelings; when the mind is going to despair, it needs a
> solace of affection and kindness. (B. H. Roberts, *A Comprehensive*

History of The Church of Jesus Christ of Latter-day Saints, 2nd ed. [Salt Lake City: The Church of Jesus Christ of Latter-day Saints, 1949] 4:606-7.)

There is no home without love. You may have a palace and yet not have a home, and you may live in a log house with a dirt roof and a dirt floor, and have there the most glorious home in all the world, if within those four log walls there permeates the divine principles of love . . . (David O. McKay, *Pathways to Happiness,* [Salt Lake City: Bookcraft, 1957], p. 114.)

The Lord, however, cautioned against jealousy of a man's role. "Murmur not" was his counsel to Emma.

President Hugh B. Brown wrote to us:

The work in the home, as well as in the Church, requires that women, as stated, shall stand side by side with their husbands, not in front of them, not behind them. While by divine decree man is to be the head of the house and the bearer of the priesthood, women are to become joint inheritors, equal partners and custodians with men in all that God has promised to the faithful. (*Continuing the Quest,* [Salt Lake City: Deseret Book Company 1961], p. 4.)

The dominion, then, is to be a joint dominion, and the command to multiply and replenish the earth is necessarily a joint injunction. When the Lord made provision for men to have the priesthood and gave the sacred honor and glory of motherhood to women, he divided not only the responsibilities but the blessings of life equally between men and women.

As Sharon's understanding increased over the years the fright and anger receded. In its place came a true appreciation of the power of the plan of life and salvation. She began to accept the challenges of walking side by side with her husband in cooperation and serenity. She was satisfied in her heart that the priesthood was not given to man that he might subjugate woman—rather, it was a power delegated to bless the lives of all men and women, all of God's children everywhere.

She feels the peaceful strength of that blessing now.

9

Reach for the Stars

Few people are untouched today by economic stress. We're not only confronted with it in the media, but we experience it with virtually every purchase we make.

Most Saturday afternoons my husband and I make a trip to the grocery store for our weekly supplies and food storage items. Recently, after filling our shopping cart and while waiting to be checked out, we watched the cashier totaling the purchases of customers ahead of us. Nearly all were in sizable double-digit figures. We discussed the high cost of food for large families with limited incomes, elderly people with small pensions, and single parents often with uncertain means. We concluded that in most households resources must be managed very carefully in order to meet current demands.

The economic situation today is sobering. It requires us as women to be very resourceful, if we are to meet this challenge successfully and at the same time find satisfaction in doing it well.

A young bride went to be with her husband at an army camp on the edge of a desert. Housing was scarce and costly. All they could afford was a small cabin near an Indian village. The 115-degree heat was unbearable in the daytime. The wind blew constantly, spreading dust and sand over everything. The days were long and lonely. When her husband was ordered into the desert for two weeks of maneuvers, she just couldn't bear the living conditions any longer, and she wrote to her mother that she was coming home. An almost immediate reply included these lines:

> Two men looked out from prison bars,
> One saw mud, the other saw the stars.

She read the lines over and over. All right, she would look for the stars.

She determined to make friends with her neighbors, the Indians. She admired their artful weaving and pottery work and asked them to teach her. As soon as they sensed her genuine interest, they were most willing. She became fascinated with their culture, their history—everything about them. The desert changed from a desolate, forbidding place to a world of wondrous beauty.

What had changed? Not the desert, not her environment; her own attitude transformed a miserable experience into a highly rewarding one.

How might a woman look to the stars to create an environment of optimism and adventure, while at the same time stretching her dollars and resources by implementing sound economic principles in the home?

Wise home and money management instruction is available to help each sister learn how to bring all expenditures within the family income. It has been thoughtfully said that we should set our scale of living one degree below our means. No longer can we ignore the imperative of this principle.

The first hard rule of fixing our scale of living below our means is to budget, planning first for basic needs and then for other desirable items.

We should help all women enjoy the peace of mind that comes from making and following a plan for spending. Their lives will begin to have an aura of serenity when their expenses stay within their income.

Women must learn to budget and to help their children learn to budget also. We should all know that, no matter how important or worthwhile an item might seem to be, if we cannot afford it, it is an unwise expenditure. Such expenditures lead to debt, and unwise debt leads to economic insecurity, which most often causes stress in the family. We can make it easier for children if we advise them as Elder Marvin J. Ashton suggests: " 'Save your money' is a hollow pronouncement from a parent to a child. 'Save your money for a mission, bicycle, doll house, trousseau, or car' makes understandable sense." (*Ensign,* July 1975, p. 73.)

Living on a budget is not a chore. It need not even be a deprivation. Budgeting should be a great learning experience.

A recently married daughter of a friend wrote her mother, describing how she and her husband were managing to save money on their meager income. She excitedly explained: "I've discovered that often prepared foods are too costly for our budget, so I make most things from scratch. The other night at Relief Society I even learned how to make milk, buttermilk, condensed milk, cottage cheese, yogurt, and cream cheese from the powdered milk we had stored. It's fun to see how much I can save by doing things myself."

We must be realistic in money management and still maintain a spirit of resourcefulness and optimism. For example: car pool or walk whenever possible, wear sweaters, turn down the thermostat a degree or two, open shades when the sun shines and close them at night, turn off the heat or air conditioner when not at home, turn off the lights, and run the dishwasher only with a full load.

Resource management should include wise stewardship of possessions and an appreciation of the value that still remains in some used goods. One stake Relief Society president reported on a homemaking meeting they had held with the best seamstress available to help each woman draft patterns for reusable fabric. This helped their sisters save many dollars and at the same time enjoy lovely additional clothing items.

Other classes on resource management focused on ways to take better care of clothes—how best to repair, clean, and alter them for longer wear. Laundering tips added to a woman's understanding of how to give longer life to fabric. Classes were offered on the art of clothing coordination, how to add variety and versatility to everyone's wardrobe so there was less need to purchase complete outfits. In these and other ways Relief Society teaches women to care better for their belongings, thus extending the serviceability of each item while at the same time bringing the owner satisfaction and pleasure.

If we "make do" creatively, we don't have to do without. We can enrich the lives of our family members at very little cost.

Save money by helping your family members maintain the best health of which they are capable. Take advantage of physical fitness training to promote well-being as the least expensive medical treatment. The illness you avoid costs nothing—not even the price of an aspirin! Good health habits save money. To promote good health, women need to plan nutritious meals. Most of us could have smaller portions of food and still be healthy, but all of us should eat regular, well-balanced meals each day, understand and practice the fundamentals of good nutrition. We should learn to prepare economical food that will be both nourishing and appealing.

We should make our homes models of provident living that can meet present needs and provide for possible emergencies.

I have thought about the emergency preparation necessary when Noah's ark was made ready. Noah must have achieved the most effective planning in the history of mankind when he very carefully followed the Lord's counsel and built the ark. His wife and their sons undoubtedly worked and planned with him so that the blessings of the Lord might be theirs. Just think of preparing a year's supply for those multitudes of animals which were brought into the ark. Noah and his family must have been able to plan and provide in such a way that they could find pleasure in their efforts (selecting just the right two of each kind of animal), adventure in their voyage (surely there were new, little, furry creatures almost weekly), joy as the splendor of the very first rainbow filled the sky and the Lord's promise was fulfilled.

We can meet the great challenge of economic stress by wise management of that with which the Lord has blessed us. If we look for the stars we can find satisfaction, even joy, in living.

III

Of Loving in Marriage and in Family

10

For Time and All Eternity

Some time ago, our second son took a very beautiful young woman to the Salt Lake Temple. They were married for time and all eternity. Both our son and his bride had enjoyed rich, full, single lives—so much so that my husband and I wondered if our son would ever leave his singleness and settle down to married life.

He had completed a mission, graduated from the university, and he was finishing his last year of law school. He was thoroughly enjoying his legal training. He had many friends.

His bride was a graduate of Brigham Young University and she had received her master's degree in social work from the University of Utah. She was working in the Granite School District, counseling children there. Besides her professional work, she was serving as a stake Relief Society president in one of the singles stakes. She too had many friends. She had toured Europe. She was free to do just about whatever she pleased.

They had met about two years earlier. After that, each of them had dated other people until one day he told me he had decided to ask her to marry him. I was more than delighted. She was a very special person. She had the attributes and qualifications I felt were important for a good wife in today's world, or in any time. I knew he had given the decision to marry his very best thinking. He knew it was the most important decision of his life and that he would have to live with it not only now but forever.

They both came to their marriage as individuals, sure of themselves in fundamental ways. They had the knowledge that they were each loved, honored, and respected as individuals. Each had pursued education. Each had made a start at contributing meaningfully from personal insights and training.

When they were married I had another concern. What kind of an eternal relationship would they have with each other? Would they live happily forever after?

Handsome young men and beautiful young women always do in fairy tales. But I knew, and so did they, that marriage is no fairy tale. It is hard, real, everyday living—the routine of making beds, doing dishes, preparing meals, cutting lawns, shoveling snow. It is earning enough money to have the basic necessities to sustain life: food, clothing, shelter. It is paying for light, heat, telephone, and for taxes.

Living is problems to solve and responsibilities to accept. It is babies to bear and nurture. Those babies grow into teenagers. Teenagers grow into adults, and at every stage of their development, each has problems.

Living together is learning how to communicate with someone who thinks, feels, and acts differently than you do. It is planning and achieving, seeking and striving, and it is growing together.

Married life is an everyday kind of business, trying to meet the needs of one another and a family. But that is the only way a couple could have a successful marriage.

As they began their married life together, I couldn't help but wonder what kind of an arrangement they would choose for their pattern of living.

They could pattern their lives like so many big corporations that buy smaller companies. They merge their assets and liabilities. The small company loses its identity. The big company becomes stronger and its power increases until it is able to compete in the most ambitious markets, but the small company is as if it never existed.

Too many marriages are like that. One or the other partner no longer has any identity. The effectiveness of the lost partner is minimal.

Perhaps, they would form, as do some small companies, an unequal partnership where one partner owns the controlling stock in the company. The largest stockholder becomes the dominant, deciding force. We have some friends who have had that kind of a business arrangement. One partner made most of the decisions, did most of the work, and finally it became a quarrelsome enterprise and the partnership was dissolved.

I hope that doesn't happen to them.

Too many marriages use this model and do not utilize the strengths of either the husband or the wife. These marriages often end in unhappiness, a disaster for the entire family that was started with happiness and hope.

I suppose what I would like to see is my son and daughter-in-law as equal partners in their marriage relationship. Both would bring their assets and liabilities, their teachings, testimonies, educational and professional background, their healthy vibrant spirits, good bodies and minds, their evaluative understanding to help them recognize truth so they would "reason together" and make the most of what each has to offer.

In that way they can learn to function as equal partners, both helping to make decisions with a clear, healthy vision of what each thinks and why, so they can come to a consensus of opinion cooperatively together. They would then be prepared to fulfill their individual roles and function well together in their joint roles. When he speaks he will know that she will support him and that he can confidently speak for both of them. She will also feel free to express an opinion or make a commitment for both of them because she would know his feelings about their plans; they will be able to work together as one.

It seems to me that in the equal partnership they will find

all the pleasures of individual opportunities within the strength of unity that comes from having the full support of each other.

Partnership of the man and the woman is the message of the gospel. It is a divine teaching desperately needed in a world now in the process of rewriting the relationships of men and women. The Lord has revealed some significant things over the centuries of time. He has told us of the great worth of each soul. He has said all should come unto him, "male and female." He has warned against power struggles in all their forms, telling us they are not of heaven. And he has given us instructions to work together as one, for strength comes from loving unity.

The Lord gave both of them, as husband and wife, those joint responsibilities. He also gave specific responsibilities to Adam and specific responsibilities to Eve. He said, "It is not good that the man should be alone; I will make an help meet for him" (Genesis 2:18). The Lord knew that it was not good for man to be alone—not only because he could not procreate children alone, but also because alone Adam could not assume the responsibilities necessary to help him achieve godhood.

The scriptures clearly indicate to me that Adam, like all of us, needed someone to love, someone he could serve, and someone to love him if he were to fulfill the purpose of his creation. And Eve was to be the one to help bring about that glorious purpose.

Neither could Eve learn what she had to learn alone. It was part of the eternal plan that they would need each other—that they would work together in harmony, in love, in sacrifice, to experience learning in mortality.

In the true patriarchal order man holds the priesthood and is the head of the household of faith, but he cannot attain a fulness of joy here or of eternal rewards hereafter alone. Woman stands at his side, a joint-inheritor with him in the fulness of times. Exaltation and eternal increase is her lot as well as his. Godhood is not only for men; it is for men and women together. It is "to *their* exaltation and glory in all things." (See D&C 132:19-20.)

If we are to understand the significant role of the man and the woman we must understand that only together can they obtain godhood.

Some husbands and some wives claim to understand this principle and still they fail to realize how important it is that they work and plan together. If they do not communicate and help each other and grow in love, faith, and understanding, they will never enjoy the blessings promised the faithful by the Lord.

If a man uses his priesthood power unrighteously and dictates, demeans, or demands obedience, the Lord says that priesthood will be withdrawn.

> That the rights of the priesthood are inseparably connected with the powers of heaven, and that the powers of heaven cannot be controlled nor handled only upon the principles of righteousness.
>
> That they may be conferred upon us, it is true; but when we undertake to cover our sins, or to gratify our pride, our vain ambition, or to exercise control or dominion or compulsion upon the souls of the children of men, in any degree of unrighteousness, behold, the heavens withdraw themselves; the Spirit of the Lord is grieved; and when it is withdrawn, Amen to the priesthood or the authority of that man.
>
> Behold, ere he is aware, he is left unto himself, to kick against the pricks, to persecute the saints, and to fight against God. (D&C 121:36-38.)

It is in this spirit that we understand the eternal marriage covenant. It is in this spirit we must work out the daily events of family building. It brings with it the spark of fresh imagination that can transform a task into a regenerative experience. Such an experience was described to me recently by a friend:

"My wife and I decided to face the front of our home with rocks. So I called around and located a place where I could get them. I started to get into my truck when my wife called to me and said, 'Let me go with you and help you get the rocks.' I love to have her with me and so I was pleased.

"When we arrived at the place where the rocks were located, we found them on top of a hill. I complained 'What a job! That will be really tough to get all of those rocks down here and loaded into the truck.'

"My wife said, 'You stay here. I'll go up to the top of the hill and roll the rocks down to you. Then, you'll just have to carry them over to the truck. How does that sound?' I thought it was a good idea. I watched her climb to the top of the hill and disappear for a few minutes.

"Soon she called out, 'Look out, dear. Here comes the first one.'

"Then another and another. 'Oh, Bob,' she exclaimed, 'This one has real character.' Then, 'You'll love this one. Here's my favorite. I hope this one isn't too heavy for you to carry.'

"Believe me, I was determined I could carry anything she could roll down. She actually had me anxiously waiting for each rock.

"I enjoyed getting those rocks. I had thought it would be such a job. But, when my bride of over thirty years came down into that meadow that afternoon I fell in love with her all over again. I loved being there where she was surrounded by the beauties of nature. I loved thinking back over the years to the classes she had taken in sculpturing so that she could do busts of our five children. I loved the fact that she had made an intensive study of food and nutrition in order to make us a healthier, happier family. I thought of the many times I sat beside her in church. All of these experiences were ones of interest and joy beyond what I would have known without her. She had expanded my life far beyond what it could have possibly been without her."

A good blending of talents and strength comes from equal partnerships. In fact, it is more than the sum of two. The strengths of partners are compounded into a creative force of unlimited magnitude when the creative interactions begin to take place. It happens as two strong partners give willingly to each other. The creative explosions are many and varied and the atmosphere of confident faith in the power to do and to accomplish is constantly renewed. The powerful forward thrust is augmented time and time again by the creative interplay between two partners of equal worth.

This beneficial power comes in marriages as two people build a family together. It spreads to the others who are part of that family unit. This is the pattern the Lord has ordained for his church on earth, and that spirit of willing, cooperative partnership keeps the building of the kingdom going forward.

The vital need for both the man and the woman in the Church was made very clear to me one Sunday morning when I attended a sacrament service as a visitor in Honolulu. I hadn't been there very long before I could sense a restlessness and an uncertainty that was different than other times when I had been there. Then a friend, noticing my awareness that something was different, said: "The International Women's Year meeting is being held today at the high school and many of the adult women have been excused from this meeting to attend that meeting and participate."

He continued: "We can't tell you how much we miss the sisters. Ordinarily they play the organ and conduct the music. The men who are filling in for them haven't made the same preparations that they do. Those who are teaching didn't even think about sitting with the classes and so we are experiencing more confusion and irreverence among the children than we ordinarily have. No one even thought the rolls should be passed out. This is the most graphic lesson I have ever had to teach me how much we need both the men and the women in the Church."

In countless ways and in diverse organizational patterns, the women work with the men of the Church. Both are needed. In fact, President N. Eldon Tanner clearly outlined the partnership role in 1976: "The presidency of the Relief Society, having a specific responsibility placed upon them by the President of the Church at the time they were organized, should be considered as a partner with the Melchizedek Priesthood in somewhat the same manner as a wife would work with the family in directing the affairs of the family." (*Church News*, June 5, 1976, p. 3.)

And at the first special fireside for women, President Spencer W. Kimball said: "When we speak of marriage as a partnership, let us speak of marriage as a full partnership. We do not want our

LDS women to be silent partners or limited partners in that eternal assignment! Please be a contributing and full partner." (*Ensign*, 1978, p. 106.)

It seems to me their wise direction is a restatement of counsel given by the Lord in other dispensations.

In the first period of mortal time when Adam and Eve were placed on earth and instructed of the Lord, the fact of their companionship and their partnership was clearly established. In both the Pearl of Great Price (Moses 2:28) and the Bible (Genesis 1:28) —and I think the words there are significant—the Lord said: "And I, God, blessed them, and said unto them; Be fruitful, and multiply, and replenish the earth, and subdue it . . ."

And thus God, our Father, set into motion the plan for eternal growth and progress of his children. Essential instructions were given to them—both male and female—and President Kimball has explained that the word *man* as used in the scriptures relating to those instructions refers to both the man and the woman.

The teachings of the gospel make clear to us the essential nature of the eternal partnership upon which the man and the woman embark.

When Adam and Eve were driven out of the Garden of Eden, the scriptures tell us, "Adam began to till the earth . . . and Eve, also, his wife, did labor with him" (Moses 5:1).

In the beginning of this dispensation the men and women who gathered to Zion to establish the kingdom of God on earth labored side by side—doing all needful things in order to make their dreams come true.

When the Saints were forced to leave Nauvoo, the city beautiful, they were buoyed up by the great faith and a willingness to keep going.

From the inspired lyrics of "Because of Elizabeth," the Relief Society Nauvoo Pageant, came these words:

> "No despair and no self-pity,
> We are going west.
> Build another holy city,
> We're going west."

And that's just what our grandparents and great-grandparents did. They worked together to build another "holy city."

The founding of Zion in this dispensation required the vision of the chosen prophet. It also required the hard work and commitment of dedicated men and women who accepted the word of the Lord as given through him.

A prominent LDS historian, Leonard Arrington, has pointed out that subduing this arid Great Basin land required the active sacrifice and commitment of Zion's sons and daughters—and often holding the towns and preserving the communities depended on the heroic work of the women because the men were called to go on missions to preach the gospel. Crops had to be planted, cows had to be milked, harvests had to be gathered in while the men were away, and the women, as full partners in the building of the kingdom, did what had to be done.

Today we are in a new chapter of the continuing story of the challenge of helping the work of the Lord roll forth among the children of men. And it will take our best efforts—both men and women working together in full partnership—to make the gospel light shine out to all the world.

The divine counsel to work as equal partners would be the most satisfying pattern for the world to follow as well. Women have much to contribute to society. Men have much to give. Society needs the best that each individual has in order to meet its great ongoing challenges. The full partnership concept will release in our communities unlimited power for good.

No challenge is beyond the reach of good men and women working together in the patterns of service and love given by the Lord. Let us value each other, honor each other, and encourage the contributions of our differing perspectives. The dynamics of the abundant life are waiting upon our purposeful choice to be partners with each other and the Lord.

11
The Eternal Family

I went to the fortieth reunion of my high school graduating class. It had been a long time in the preparation and the arrangements were graciously and thoughtfully carried out. I had looked forward with great anticipation to the event.

I wanted to see the friends of my youth. I wondered what had become of them. I had completely lost touch with most of them. Some I could hardly wait to see. I wondered what they would be like now. Would I remember them? Would I recognize the same characteristics in their personalities that I had grown to love in the years so long ago? Would they still remember me? Would we feel warm and sharing or would the years have put a gulf between us?

When we arrived at the reunion, the committee in charge greeted us and gave us special name tags that had our yearbook pictures on them. We could see how we had looked when we went to South High School. I thought that would solve part of my problem. I knew if I could see the picture I would at least remember the face. I might even be able to catch the name before I had to reveal that I had forgotten my friends. At least that was the theory.

Unfortunately, I didn't have time to go thoroughly prepared, so there was a lot of anxiety and anticipation as these former classmates began coming from everywhere across the United States.

It wasn't simple returning to my high school days, but it was exciting. The people introduced themselves to each other and they told us what life had been like in the intervening years. They told us about their work, their activities, their marital status; some were married, others divorced, and then there were those who had never married. We were reminded of some who had passed on.

One man came up to me and asked that dreaded question, "Do you remember me?" My ready smile was there but my mind didn't recall a familiar face. And then he gave me his name. I should have remembered him. We had dated many times. But the truth is I didn't even recognize him, he had changed so much.

So we talked and laughed and reminisced. All of us there were sharing experiences and really concerned about those who didn't come. Where were they? What were they doing?

As I was reading in the Doctrine and Covenants it occurred to me that that gathering might be a little like our reunion will be in the spirit world. Here is the joyful description of that reunion:

> And there were gathered together in one place an innumerable company of the spirits of the just, who had been faithful in the testimony of Jesus while they lived in mortality; . . .

> I beheld that they were filled with joy and gladness, and were rejoicing together because the day of their deliverance was at hand. . . .

> Their sleeping dust was to be restored unto its perfect frame, bone to his bone, and the sinews and the flesh upon them, the spirit and the body to be united never again to be divided, that they might receive a fulness of joy.

> While this vast multitude waited and conversed, rejoicing in the hour of their deliverance from the chains of death, the Son of God appeared, declaring liberty to the captives who had been faithful; . . .

> Among the great and mighty ones who were assembled in this vast congregation of the righteous were Father Adam, the Ancient of Days and father of all,

And our glorious Mother Eve, with many of her faithful daughters who had lived through the ages and worshiped the true and living God. (D&C 138:12, 15, 17-18, 38-39.)

I'm looking forward to that reunion too. In a way, I'm like the little boy in the Sunday School class. The teacher asked her students if they wanted to go to heaven. The response was enthusiastic and almost universal. All the children raised their hands except for one little boy.

"What's the matter, Johnny, don't you want to go to heaven sometime?" she asked.

"Oh, yes," he said. "I want to go sometime. I just don't want to go right now. I thought you were getting up a tour or something."

I'm not interested in an immediate tour either. But sometime I hope to earn my way back to that heavenly home from whence I came, and when I get there I hope to participate in that reunion joyfully where bodies and spirits will be restored and united, never to be separated again, and ready for the next great adventure of our eternal progression. And I want you to be there too!

And as I stand, in that great reunion, or sit and talk with Mother Eve and others who are gathered there, I suspect I will find a lot of the same thoughts coming back to my mind that I thought during my high school reunion.

How wonderful it is to see all you dear, dear people again! The gratitude and the humility of being with loved ones again must be an overwhelming feeling. There are some I can't wait to see.

My mother—she who made life so much fun to live. I can still see her there in our kitchen. I can hear her laugh—and I can hear her say, "It isn't any challenge to fix a meal if you have everything to start with—the real trick comes when you make a delicious dinner from nothing." And then she really would cook a dinner that was delicious to me.

I will love to see my grandmothers—I think of both of them with great fondness.

I like to recall one particular Thanksgiving Day in about 1930. I was a little girl. Mother and Daddy had piled all six of us children into the family Model T Ford about 4:00 A.M. and we were off to our grandparents' home in Lyman, Wyoming, for the celebration. We sped along, sometimes at thirty miles an hour. "Dee! You're taking our lives in your hands going so fast!" I recall hearing my mother anxiously plead with my father. "Slow down; don't travel at such a high rate of speed."

As we traveled, we sang songs, played games, and listened to stories; Mother was a marvelous storyteller. It took us about eight hours to arrive at the big, old, beautiful farmhouse. Grandma and Grandpa, and all of Daddy's brothers and sisters and their families, came rushing out of the house to greet us with hugs and kisses. We felt welcomed and loved as we were ushered into the big dining room. I'll never forget seeing the big dining room table extended across the room and then additional tables placed through the rest of the dining room and through the full length of the front room. That year fifty of us sat down together for our traditional Thanksgiving dinner. I remember the happy feeling I had that day as I looked down that long table and thought, "Each person here is related to me." It gave me a feeling of pride knowing that they were good, kind, happy people.

I think fondly of my maternal grandmother, who was a practicing physician and surgeon. When Mother gave birth to my third brother we went to Wyoming so Nana, as we lovingly called her, could take care of Mother. After the baby was born, Nana had an emergency call so she took my older brother and me with her on the house call. We were told to wait in the car. We waited and waited for what seemed like hours. Finally the children who lived at that home invited us to come and play with them. We did, and when we happened around the side of the house, there sat my grandmother by the window bathing a brand-new baby. She laughed and I later heard her telling someone that she looked up because suddenly the light was dimmed and she saw the window full of little faces watching her.

I want her to know how much I admire her courage, her intellect, and her indomitable spirit.

I could go on and on telling you about my father, mother-in-law, father-in-law, aunts, uncles, cousins, and dear friends, but when all these first greetings and reminiscing are over, I imagine if I make it, there will come the lonesome feeling of some who are missing. Why? What happened? Why didn't they get there? Wasn't anyone there to reach out a helping hand when they needed it? How did they lose their way?

And then there will be the inevitable, what about the time since I left this place? How did I use it? When I became converted did I indeed turn to strengthen my brothers and sisters and all of my associates?

In the midst of all that happy talk there will be the quiet, deep, inner contemplation—there has to be. In that evaluation I will have to consider how I responded to the experiences of my earthly home and how I extended myself to meet the needs and situations of those who depended upon me.

There seem to be two major directions that come to us from the Lord. They are the firm footings of his gospel of glad news. I hope each one of us is converted to those two major directions.

First, I hope that I am converted to the reality of God and the consequent ordering of life that that knowledge brings. God is our Father. We are his children. Eternal progression is our birthright. All the people in the world are part of the great eternal family. Truman Madsen said:

> You have come literally "trailing clouds of glory." No amount of mortal abuse can quench the divine spark. If you only knew who you are and what you did and how you earned the privileges of mortality, and not just mortality but of this time, this place, this dispensation, and the associates that have been meant to cross and intertwine with your lives; . . .
>
> Joseph Smith taught that we cannot receive more until we honor what has already been given. We have great gifts, greater endowments, and the greatest of destinies. (*The Highest in Us* [Salt Lake City, Bookcraft, 1978], pp. 12, 20.)

God has sent his gospel to all the world through his beloved Son and through devoted servants. That good news is to help us attain the greatest of destinies.

Second, I hope each one of us is converted to the glad tidings of the gospel plan.

This means being converted to the understanding that free agency is an eternal law. We must choose to live by the light of the gospel if we are to find our way back to the holy habitation of our eternal parents.

We are the only ones who can prevent ourselves from being part of God's family forever. He will not disclaim us. He will not cast us out. But we can choose to keep ourselves from his presence.

Let me share the story told by Elder James E. Talmage called "The Parable of the Bee."

Sometimes I find myself under obligations of work requiring quiet and seclusion such as neither my comfortable office nor the cozy study at home insures. My favorite retreat is an upper room in the tower of a large building, well removed from the noise and confusion of the city streets. The room is somewhat difficult of access, and relatively secure against human intrusion. Therein I have spent many peaceful and busy hours with books and pen.

I am not always without visitors, however, especially in the summertime; for, when I sit with windows open, flying insects occasionally find entrance and share the place with me. These self-invited guests are not unwelcome. Many a time I have laid down the pen, and, forgetful of my theme, have watched with interest the activities of these winged visitants, with an after-thought that the time so spent had not been wasted, for, is it not true, that even a butterfly, a beetle, or a bee, may be a bearer of lessons to the receptive student?

A wild bee from the neighboring hills once flew into the room; and at intervals during an hour or more I caught the pleasing hum of its flight. The little creature realized that it was a prisoner, yet all its efforts to find the exit through the partly opened casement failed. When ready to close up the room and leave, I threw the window wide, and tried at first to guide and then to drive the bee to liberty and safety, knowing well that if left in the room it would die as other insects there entrapped had perished in the dry atmosphere of the enclosure. The more I tried to drive it out, the more determinedly did it oppose and resist my efforts. Its erstwhile peaceful hum developed into an angry roar; its darting flight became hostile and threatening.

Then it caught me off my guard and stung my hand—the hand

that would have guided it to freedom. At last it alighted on a pendant attached to the ceiling, beyond my reach of help or injury. The sharp pain of its unkind sting aroused in me rather pity than anger. I knew the inevitable penalty of its mistaken opposition and defiance; and I had to leave the creature to its fate. Three days later I returned to the room and found the dried, lifeless body of the bee on the writing table. It had paid for its stubbornness with its life.

To the bee's short-sightedness and selfish misunderstanding I was a foe, a persistent persecutor, a mortal enemy bent on its destruction; while in truth I was its friend, offering it ransom of the life it had put in forfeit through its own error, striving to redeem it, in spite of itself, from the prison-house of death and restore it to the outer air of liberty.

Are we so much wiser than the bee that no analogy lies between its unwise course and our lives? We are prone to contend, sometimes with vehemence and anger, against the adversity which after all may be the manifestation of superior wisdom and loving care, directed against our temporary comfort for our permanent blessing. In the tribulations and sufferings of mortality there is a divine ministry which only the godless soul can wholly fail to discern. To many the loss of wealth has been a boon, a providential means of leading or driving them from the confines of selfish indulgence to the sunshine and the open, where boundless opportunity waits on effort. Disappointment, sorrow, and affliction may be the expression of an all-wise Father's kindness.

Consider the lesson of the unwise bee!

> "Trust in the Lord with all thine heart; and lean not unto thine own understanding. In all thy ways acknowledge him, and he shall direct thy paths." (Proverbs 3:5-6.) (*Improvement Era*, September 1914.)

Sometimes we are very much like the bee. Sometimes we cannot be led. We will not be instructed. And we react violently, negatively, to all that comes to us. Such behavior can lead to stopping our eternal progress. It can leave us dead in spirit as well as body and then we will not have that time of joyful reunion. The reunion would go on but we would not be there.

I remember the nurturing I received as a child at home. I am grateful for it because it has set my feet firmly upon a good pathway. I learned there to accept the fundamentals of the gospel plan. I found there that it is possible to take a positive look at life and the world around me. Life is much more peaceful and happy when we live by gospel principles and do so with a positive attitude. The Lord tells us to have faith, hope, and charity.

Charity is scarcely possible if we do not have faith and hope. Hope leads us to faith and a deep faith can lead us to exercise charity—the pure love of Christ.

Hope in the scriptural sense requires that we look for the positive use of life's experiences. We were never promised that living a Christlike life would prevent us from having sorrow and pain and adversity. What we are promised is that if we live with faith and hope and charity, good will come from each of life's experiences. It cannot fail. It is God's love. It is perfect love.

Many times the only difference between disaster and the creation of something valuable is the way the circumstances are viewed. Many a women today has found in the gospel the inspiration to set herself on the upward, learning, loving course that the Lord tells us will lead to eternal life.

We will find the light we need in the scriptures and in the words of the modern prophets. We will find the strength we need to apply those principles in constant secret prayer. We will find the growth we need in living the principles of truth. Where do we start? "Let's start at the very beginning," the song says, "a very good place to start!"

When Jesus was asked, "Master, which is the great commandment in the law?"

> Jesus said unto him, Thou shalt love the Lord thy God with all thy heart, and with all thy soul, and with all thy mind.
> This is the first and great commandment.
> And the second is like unto it, Thou shalt love thy neighbor as thyself. (Matthew 22:37-39.)

Questioned further, and in summary just before he left the earth, the Lord said: "Verily I say unto you, Inasmuch as ye have done it unto the least of these my brethren, ye have done it unto me." (Matthew 25:40.)

A careful examination of the scriptures show us that he is talking about service to one another—and not particularly great service. He is talking about performing acts of compassionate service to all with whom we come in contact: visiting the fatherless, seeing those in prison, caring for the needy, giving comfort to those who mourn, feeding the hungry, listening to the toubled heart, giving water to those who thirst. At some time he will come in glory, but up to this point his example and his teaching have been to bring our attention to the small, everyday wants and needs of those who surround us. Our place at the great reunion will be earned by day-to-day acts of compassionate service.

In the Book of Mormon, counsel is given for those who do not have enough to give. He says that if they desire to impart of their substance then their progress will continue, for they desired to do that which was right. I feel confident that he was referring to people like a sister I met in a rest home in Lethbridge, Canada.

I was invited to visit Barbara Gotee by her stake Relief Society president. Barbara had been in the hospital for years. She had been in an automobile accident when she and her husband and son were on their way to sacrament meeting. They were anxious to hear their son report his mission. A truck struck them and both her son and husband were killed. She was badly cut and left paralyzed from the neck down. That accident occurred many years ago.

When I asked her how she was, she said, "Spiritually I'm just fine. I have a good place to live, good care, wonderful visiting teachers I couldn't do without, and I know that the Lord lives and loves me."

I can't help but shed a few tears as I think of her courage, her appreciation, and her great faith. All of these character traits continued to grow, and under such adverse conditions—for she faced not only the tragedy of death but the reality of life without the use of her body. Her giving was word, not deed. She did not judge others. She knew that Jesus told us not to judge one another. Very specifically he says to give to the beggar even if his condition was brought on by unrighteousness. It is not for us to judge one another but rather to reach out and strengthen, to give comfort, and to love as needed. (See Mosiah 4:17.)

The perfecting of ourselves is an ongoing process. We learn by doing. We do it one step at a time. We search out ways to give service and to share our lives with others, and then we grow. It is as simple as it sounds. If we reached out to those around us, and each of them reached out, we would soon have love unfeigned governing us and that would bring us closer to our goal of reunion as an eternal family.

To become part of his family eternally does not require monumental achievements as recognized by the world, although he does not scorn them either. What he does ask of us is a humble spirit and a contrite heart so that we might remain teachable forever. This is desirable because, as promised, "Be thou humble; and the Lord thy God shall lead thee by the hand, and give thee answer to thy prayers." (D&C 112:10.) What a magnificent promise!

I believe that we are entitled to the promptings of the still small voice to help us make decisions and to guide our actions day by day. The still small voice is not a trumpet nor a great, overpowering sound or power. It is a quiet, still, and gentle voice, yet it pierces the soul. President Marion G. Romney once said that when he went to stake conferences he always tried to arrive a little time before the others came so that he could become quiet and be prepared to listen to the promptings of the still small voice. We too need a quiet time to listen.

When I contemplate that great time of rejoicing when the family of the Son of Man shall gather with the Ancient of Days and Mother Eve and all who have come on earth to be teachers of his holy word, I am sure we shall look for our family members and we shall pray that they will be among the number.

As a mother, I pray each day that I may be successful in teaching and sustaining my children and my grandchildren that they may come and join with me and my husband and that together we may be worthy to be in that heavenly congregation.

As a woman, I am grateful that the Lord has given me the privilege of bearing children and thus giving his eternal offspring an opportunity for mortality.

As a woman—both as a mother and as a woman in the kingdom of God—I have been entrusted with many opportunities to help make life worth living for all with whom I come in contact. I pray that I might be able to expand and enlarge my skills in this direction.

As a woman called to service in the Church, I pray constantly that my efforts will expand the horizons for others who are converted and who come looking for strength and continued vision.

The Relief Society is the home of the Lord's program for his daughters, and I pray that it may be a useful tool for all of us to learn compassionate service, to strengthen our own testimonies and those of others, and to share righteousness in our sisterhood with concern and love. Let us reach out for all the good things of life. Let us individually seek ways to grow and expand. Let us use the scriptures and the teachings of the prophets to prepare us so that the light of the gospel may shine in our lives.

And then when it is time for us each to lay this mortal by, we can look forward to that grand, eternal, family reunion in the heavens when we shall meet our Father and Mother in their royal courts on high.

12

Her Children Arise Up, and Call Her Blessed

In Proverbs, King Lemuel speaks of what his mother taught him. She gave him such an impressive guide that it is recorded in great detail. She made a particular point of telling him about the qualities and attitudes to look for in a wife and in the mother of his children if his household were to be so well managed that in the end the children would arise up and call their mother blessed. (See Proverbs 31:28.)

We need this kind of specific counsel in this day when so many avenues of interest are open to women, and when more and more opportunities are coming to us. We need to look very closely not only at the offerings, but at our own family's needs, if finally our children will receive here in mortality the eternal blessings that a mother is so ably qualified to give.

Each mother will have to determine how she can bless her children. Because of the many options from which a woman might choose, it becomes extremely important that she select carefully.

To the woman with children at home, that choice becomes not only important but critical. She will need unerring sources for direction—the scriptures, the teachings of Church leaders, and personal affirmation to her prayers of supplication. The changing winds of which we are warned in Ephesians (4:14) are perhaps nowhere more apparent than in the challenges and decisions women are facing now.

We could be easily "tossed to and fro" (Ephesians 4:14) if it were not for the "more sure word of prophecy; whereunto ye do well that ye take heed, as unto a light that shineth in a dark place." (2 Peter 1:19.)

In that light of truth each woman can walk with confidence, knowing what is right for her. There is no one way that will fit all circumstances. Some women must come to one solution and some to another.

The ideal for a family is, and always has been, to have a mother in the home to be with the children, to care for them and to help them grow, to coordinate and correlate the family's activities, and to be a stay against intrusions of unrighteousness. There are times, however, under unusual circumstances, when in order to help provide for even the basic needs of her family a mother may be required to accept employment outside her home. As President Ezra Taft Benson has stated, "Many of you find yourselves in circumstances that are not always ideal . . . who, because of necessity, must work and leave your children with others." (*Ensign,* November 1981, p. 105.)

Those mothers, in spite of their added working role, still must provide the emotional support that children need. In addition to the obvious physical needs of children, there are other aspects of a child's life that should not be neglected.

The challenges facing the working mother of small children are many. First, she must find someone to give good care to her child. Next, she has to decide what to do in an emergency situation when there is an accident or sickness. She must rely on the help of an understanding employer, or a relative, a neighbor, a school teacher, or someone to help in those times of crisis.

Most working mothers organize their time by advance planning, shopping, scheduling, and assigning chores to include each member of the household. They realize the importance of having meals that provide essential nutrients and the warmth of gracious family dining even though fast food establishments appeal to and even cater to the working-outside-the-home mother as an easier alternative.

The real challenges, however, for many working mothers come in their responsibility for guiding children through periods of questioning and of decision making and in their times of trouble. These challenges come in being able to sense the unexpressed needs of children and those about which young people, in their immaturity, may not themselves be aware—and sensing these needs during a much more limited amount of shared time. An employed mother may not always be on hand when her child's needs seem most acute. We find that many working mothers are very conscientious and they take every opportunity to be with their children. They work with their children in accomplishing household duties. When it is appropriate they shop, plan, and play together, and sometimes, they make a special effort to just be in the same room so that their children have the sense of being with someone who loves them.

It might be a temptation for a working mother to plan special outings and play times as the so-called "quality" time she has with her children. Many are aware of the danger this poses in giving their children a distorted picture of life by using all their time together in recreation. It is important for children to see the balance that is necessary between work and play. They need to know that special events are more meaningful when daily routines are established and when assigned duties are completed.

Grandmother Winifred Smith helped our children learn this truth. When they went to her house she was careful to have jobs they could do together; then afterward they played a game. Then they did another task, followed again by a game. The children learned, as she hoped they would, the relationship between work and play and the comfortable sense of playing after work is completed.

School work, too, and practicing to develop musical or other talents can become part of the daily routine. A mother who strives to know success can help her children learn the price of success by working with them, when necessary, to help them reach a degree of excellence. A mother can make the difference in a child's achievement. She can give support by monitoring the completion and the accuracy of assignments. She can help a child reap the rewards of persistent effort.

Even though a working mother cannot be the full-time model she might be if she were home with her children, she can help them learn the personal discipline that comes with daily, routine responsibilities, and afterwards, the well-being resulting from praise for work well done.

A mother must consider the essential purposes of life. Leo Rosten—writer, scientist, professor—has made a statement that gives us ideas to ponder:

> Where was it ever promised us that life on this earth would ever be easy, free from conflict and uncertainty, devoid of anguish and wonder? . . .
>
> The purpose of life is to matter, to be productive, to have it make some difference that you lived at all.
>
> Happiness, in the ancient, noble sense, means self-fulfillment—and is given to those who use to the fullest whatever talents God . . . bestowed upon them. . . .
>
> "Happiness, to me, lies in stretching, to the farthest boundaries of which we are capable, the resources of mind and heart."
>
> (*This Week* magazine, January 20, 1963, p. 2.)

A woman who must work to care for the needs of her children should learn the essential purposes of life and come to know the Lord and feel his love and direction. Then she can help her children know him and grow to feel secure in our Heavenly Father's love.

One woman who came to this realization wrote to me in these terms:

> Right after my divorce, I determined that I was going to give my children the best of everything . . . I would provide well for them . . . I would substitute in every way for their father. I would take them on picnics, build them a tree house, and play baseball with them. I would not allow them to suffer because of our divorce.
>
> I baked, sewed, ran, played, wrestled. I cleaned, I ironed. I was busy being both mother and father for them.

One evening I put the three of them in the bathtub together while I finished a chore. Then I came back, soaped the youngest, rinsed him off, lifted him from the tub and stood him on a bath mat while I wrapped a bath towel around him. Then I carried him off to the bedroom to put his pajamas on and tuck him into bed. I repeated the process with his brother and sister.

As I bent down to kiss them goodnight, my older son said, "Sing us a song, please."

"Which one?" I asked.

" 'Rudolph!' " said the youngest immediately.

"No, 'Johnny Appleseed,' " said his brother.

Then their sister said, "Sing, 'Stay Awake.' "

"I can see if I stay to sing one song, I'll be singing for an hour, and I don't have an hour to spare. So goodnight." I turned off the lights.

"Please sing just one song, Mommy. You can choose the song."

"What about our prayers?"

Firmly, I replied, "I said goodnight and I mean goodnight."

As I walked back to the bathroom to tidy up, I thought of how grateful they would be someday when they were old enough to understand how much I had done for them!

As I entered the room, I stopped short. There on the bath mat were three perfect sets of damp footprints. For one brief moment I thought I saw standing in the footprints the spirits of those precious children I had just tucked into bed. In that instant I saw the foolishness of my ways. I had been so busy providing for the physical needs of their mortal bodies I was neglecting their spirits. I knew then that I had a sacred obligation to nourish both. If I were to clothe them in the latest fashions and give them all that money could buy and fail to tend to their spiritual needs, I could not justifiably account for my awesome responsibility as their mother.

Humbled, I went back to their bedroom. We knelt together in prayer. We all four climbed upon the boys' big bed and sang song after song until I was the only one awake to sing.

Latter-day Saint mothers can find programs in Relief Society that will help them meet the many needs of their children—not only their health and safety, their food and clothing, their social and emotional needs, but their spiritual growth, and the establishment of good family relationships that will last beyond time.

Testimonies abound in support of those who have provided extraordinary care as single parents. We are confident that the Lord is particularly mindful of such women, and while their role is an unusually challenging one, they can succeed. But they too must make their decisions in the light of the principles and purposes of the Lord.

With the help of the Lord, families will be given strength to do what they must do—working together, using every skill to organize and to be provident, in order that they might accomplish the goals they have set. Young children respond readily to real need and can work together with their parent or parents to achieve family success.

Of all the creations of God, men and women are the ones that are to become as he is. We are his children. He has given us a plan, a model, and teachings that will help us gain his attributes.

We can learn to become like him as we use his ways to teach our children: establishing regular communications with them, listening, guiding, prompting; watching over them always, protecting, but not manipulating; allowing them to learn by experience, correcting them in such a way that they learn to obey—not because it is our will but because they have learned to do what is right to grow in wisdom.

We can plan our lives and, to the degree that it is possible, determine the end from the beginning, by building upon God-given principles to provide the security of truth.

We can strive to be models of righteousness. Children learn what life is by observing and doing.

When a mother provides an example of joy, the children's world is one of happiness. When she makes wise choices, she helps them learn discernment. She can bring to her home the refining quality that is such an important element in worthwhile progress. Learning from the Lord a Christlike love, she can manifest this kind of selfless care that will bless her home and at the same time show her children how to love. As we are told in the scriptures, "by laboring with all the might of [our] body and the faculty of [our] whole soul," we can have peace in our lives, and we can "teach [our] children to pray, and to walk uprightly before the Lord" (Words of Mormon 1:18; D&C 68:28).

Mothers have the special opportunity of bringing children into the world. They can also play a significant role in bringing to pass their success and happiness here and as they prepare for life eternal.

The economic conditions of today present problems to women and their families that have many implications and far-reaching effects. A woman can find solutions as she recognizes the needs that only she can fill and the part that she must play in the Christlike development of her children. As she lives close to the Spirit the way will be made clear for her. A wife may be compelled to help with the finances of her family. In this matter we have been given direction. President Kimball has stated:

> Some women, because of circumstances beyond their control, must work. We understand that . . . do not, however, make the mistake of being drawn off into secondary tasks which will cause the neglect of your eternal assignments such as . . . rearing the spirit children of our Father in Heaven. Pray carefully over all your decisions. (*Ensign*, November 1979, p. 103.)

In "A Little Parable For Mothers" by Temple Bailey, a young mother setting out on her path of life was told that the way would not be easy but that the end would be better than the beginning. She taught her children that life was good. She gave them courage, fortitude, and strength. And finally she was able to teach them to look above the clouds that bring shadows of darkness into this life to see the glory of God. Knowing how to find their Heavenly Father through the darkness and living by the light of his glory, her children could walk alone. The mother's journey was over but the end was better than the beginning because of what she had been able to teach her children. (Typescript, LDS Church Historical Department, Salt Lake City, Utah.)

In the end it is you wonderful mothers—you who have put your families first, who have helped each child grow to feel the acceptance of your love and the love of our Father in Heaven, and you who have taught the truth of the gospel as your lives bear witness of it—it is you whose children will "arise up, and call [you] blessed" (Proverbs 31:28).

13
A Key to Many Family Problems

"In the beginning was the Word," or, as in the Joseph Smith Translation, "In the beginning the gospel was preached through the Son. And the gospel was the word. . . . In [the Son] was the gospel, and the gospel was the life, and the life was the light of men." (John 1:1; JST, John 1, 4.)

It is sad that not all men and women enjoy the light that was intended for them. Not all who have the gospel know how to bring its radiance into their lives.

One woman felt she had little or no light in her life. Her husband spent three days of each week traveling out of town because of his work. This left her home alone to manage their house and two small children. She was just nineteen when they were married. She had almost no experience in caring for young children, and certainly felt no confidence in handling her own. She often found their demands and the pressing household duties overwhelming. In her frustration, she grew increasingly harsh with them until her abusive behavior became frightening, even to herself. Feeling alone, ashamed, and inadequate she was often in the depths of despair. What light did the gospel offer to her?

She and her husband considered themselves good members of the Church, but what difference did that make when the children were crying, the laundry piled higher and higher, the letter from her mother remained unanswered, and the dress she was to make this week for her husband's company party lay unfinished on the sewing machine. All these frustrations spoke so loudly the discouragement of the present. They made the blessings of the gospel seem very far away.

Fortunately, there were those who helped her learn to apply the principles of the gospel in solving many of her problems. Her visiting teachers, responding to her anxiety over her children, brought a special toy for each child. They had carefully selected playthings that an adult could use with a child in a delightful but problem-solving way. They took time to show the mother how to relate to her children through activity. She was surprised to find how happy and responsive the children were. They began to look forward to a playtime association with their mother. She realized that she was providing for their needs through play, and that they were becoming more relaxed with her.

Because of the relationship they were establishing through their activities together, the children were more willing to do as she asked—to pick up their clothes, to put their toys away, and to take their naps. This, in turn, helped her have more time to organize her other responsibilities. She learned to be considerate of her children and sensitive to their concerns. She has continued giving the children this special attention each day. Love in this home is now more than a concept—it is the way family members respond to each other's needs.

The word of the gospel as it is preached and learned is, for each of us, the beginning. "Knowing" alone, however, is not always sufficient to bring the promised light. We have to live by every word. We speak often in our worldwide Church about translation. Computers are being employed to assist, and hundreds of language specialists are engaged in this important work. But the translation for which we each bear personal responsibility is converting the words of the gospel into actions, attitudes, and habits.

The gospel principle of love suggests action in the injunction "love one another." When these words are translated into a determined effort to change a behavior that brings hurt or embarrassment or sorrow to a loved one, that effort becomes a key to solving a family problem. These few lines, written by a wife to her husband, underscore the need to make a principle more than a word:

Valentine's Day 1951

Dear Bill,

I feel I love you more today than I have in all our 23 years together. Although you have always told me of your affection, nothing has so convinced me that you really care as your recent preparation to take our family to the temple.

In spite of the exciting things we have done together, there has always been, for me, a sadness, a kind of lingering unhappiness, because we weren't really one. I am filled now with great expectation and joy when I think of the closeness we can have in studying the gospel together, in sharing the same friends, and, above all, the eternities that are now possible for us with our children and their children and theirs.

My admiration for you has grown as I have seen you succeed in the difficult struggle to give up the enslaving habits that had become so much a part of you.

Your sons, your daughters, and I are not only extremely proud, but grateful too.

Love,

Ellen

Not all marital unhappiness stems from obviously bad habits. Some problems develop silently, almost imperceptibly, as we are involved in taxing schedules and multiple demands. Consider the couple who have spent all their married years in devotion to Church and children. The children are now grown and have left home; church callings are less demanding; and unexpectedly, they who have spent years helping others resolve difficulties, face problems of their own. Preoccupied with serving their children, they had forgotten to serve each other. Quick to lavish affection on those about them, they had neglected sharing simple expressions of love and concern with one another. Now, in the time when they might enjoy the richness of their experiences together, they found their relationship strained. Each felt a sense of falling short that easily led to criticism and complaint. Their years of Church activity, however, had taught them a better way. They had experienced the light of the gospel and longed for it now.

They found that by taking a fresh view of gospel principles, this time as a means of solving their own problems, they could relearn how to serve one another. They realized that expressing their affection in those mellowing years together brought a sweetness and satisfaction that was especially rewarding. They selected some projects on which they worked together around their home; they found meaningful Church activity; they prepared family records and histories; they learned how to preserve other valuable documents. Already, in the gospel, they had the principles they needed, and found them more than adequate as they brought them to bear on their own problems.

G. K. Chesterton in an essay titled "A Piece of Chalk" wrote of going into the countryside in the south of England to draw with his colored chalks—only to find, ruefully, that he was missing the color white. Being too far from a store to remedy the situation, he felt his expedition ruined until he suddenly realized that the rock upon which he sat was, in fact, white chalk.

There, in a Sussex meadow, he was "sitting on an immense warehouse of white chalk." For him to think he had no chalk was like a chemist in the middle of the ocean looking for salt water to perform experiments or someone in the vast Sahara searching for sand to fill an hourglass. Many times the solutions to our problems await only our discovery that we already have the key to the answer. The need is for us to learn to use it effectively.

We see this continually in people's lives. One example was the woman who had little money to spend but wanted to share a Christmas treat with her neighbors. She didn't feel that she could buy even inexpensive containers, but she was quite self-reliant. With what she had on hand, she made charming remembrances using brown, lunch-size paper bags decorated with a white paper roof, a door, windows, and the words "Merry Christmas, Neighbor!' These brown bag houses, filled with her home-dried apple slices, were welcome gifts. This same kind of ingenuity in working out problems with what one already has can be seen in the attractive jackets a mother made for her children out of the boys' old jeans. In each case, work, service, love, and self-reliance were the keys that opened the way for solving problems and filling needs.

Many problems are severe and debilitating. They cause fear and guilt and heartache. Often the difference in people's finding their way or discovering solutions is the kindly, understanding friendship we can provide for them. Many times it is the sympathetic arm around the shoulder and the encouraging smile that give the distressed hope and the downtrodden courage to try again. We can help them know that others wrestle with problems too, but strength of family and of character, developed through living gospel principles, has enabled them to rise above life's difficulties.

One such family was left by the father when the youngest child was four months old. It was a traumatic time with a difficult divorce, but the courageous mother was full of faith and determined that she would do everything she could to succeed as a single parent.

She found, as many do, that the gospel when translated into action not only provides a key to solving problems, it can prevent them. Difficulties that could lead to dependency can be resolved and bring, instead, strength and happiness.

This mother gathered her children about her and explained their situation. There were back payments due on the house, current bills of every sort, and no income. They *could* turn to others for help, but if they were willing to work together as a family, she thought they could keep their house and make it, once more, a happy home. They were willing. Every child who was old enough found a way to help earn some money. They cut lawns, delivered papers, tended babies, collected aluminum cans, did housework. One of the older children took the responsibility for the gas bill, another for the lights; the mother put her earnings toward the house payments. They limited other spending to bare necessities.

In time, the house payments were caught up; they were able to meet their other obligations and actually invest in some small, inexpensive properties they could fix up to generate income. This enabled the mother to be at home. With these ends achieved, the children no longer needed to contribute all their earnings to the family's physical requirements. With freedom from financial threat, the mother now suggested to her children that if they wanted to continue to work they could attend college, go on missions, and even travel and see the world together. The children did continue to earn and save their money. They learned the value of work and of family, and they have accompanied their mother to places others only dream of.

The family did all these things while fulfilling their Church obligations. They are quick to testify that the greatest reward they have received from the experiences of the past few years has been their spiritual growth. Putting such principles as love, work, service, self-reliance, and consecration into practice has brought to this family the dignity of accomplishment, a unity of purpose, and a closeness to one another and to the Lord that is immediately apparent when one is in their company.

Life does present problems, and although the gospel provides a means for finding answers, the resolutions do not always come quickly. There are, however, desirable strengths we develop by striving against difficulties. It is often when struggling to the very extremity of our power that we come to know our Father in Heaven is close.

Sariah, the wife of Lehi, had the wrenching experience of leaving their home and their possessions to travel in the wilderness. We are not told of the trials she may have experienced, but going on foot, living in tents, and cooking over an open fire could have been devastating after their comfortable life in Jerusalem. We do read of her anguished waiting when she feared her beloved sons had perished in their return to obtain the plates. But in spite of troubles, she did love and serve her family. With the return of her sons, she knew of a certainty that the Lord had commanded her husband to flee into the wilderness. It was in their safe return that she found the assurance that the Lord was with them. Their circumstances did not change. They still slept in tents, but she had joy and comfort in the knowledge that the Lord was guiding them. In that light she could carry on and meet further difficulties as they came.

For each of us, whatever our knowledge of the gospel, we can continue to learn, but learning is just the beginning. The fulness of blessings comes as we adopt the principles and live our lives by them. We are promised that when we live the principles, they will be a light unto us.

As we come to know that light, it will lead us through the mists of darkness. As we begin to bring that light into our homes, it can become a beacon to our children and their children.

14

Living After the
Manner of Happiness

Two of my grandchildren asked me to read them a story. I agreed and they handed me the Judith Viorst book *Alexander and the Terrible, Horrible, No Good, Very Bad Day.* I read it and they laughed at the series of unpleasant events that happened to Alexander from the moment he woke up with gum in his hair until he climbed back into bed at the close of the day. The final line of the book was, "My mom says some days are like that!"

I suppose we all have some terrible, horrible, no good, very bad days to contend with, but I am saddened when I read of the response to those days of uncontrollable situations that bring about growing statistics of depression and even suicide among us. It is of particular concern to me when I note that many of those discouraged and disturbed people are young adults who are contemplating self-destruction when they are right on the verge of what would be a meaningful adult life.

So it is that I want to urge that we live after a manner of happiness, for I believe that the gospel is given to us to encourage us in our lives, indeed, that the Lord actually commands us to live "after the manner of happiness" (2 Nephi 5:27). The gospel of Jesus Christ itself is good news and glad tidings. It is designed to provide us with all the tools we need to fashion for ourselves the joyful, more abundant life.

I believe that when we have religion in our lives it will give us a bearing not to be found anywhere else. I believe that the questions raised by religious teachings that confront the practices of men are very necessary questions. We each need the stimulation and the discipline that comes from vigorously pursuing the answers to the questions raised in such an exchange.

One such confrontation has to do with the concept of happiness. We hear all about us: "How boring," "What a drag each day is," and how "depraved" men and women are because of the animal nature of human beings. We must resist the inevitable conclusion of such thinking, because the good news of the gospel is that we are children of God, and being of the race of gods there is within us a divine power to do much good. God, who is our eternal Father, has sent his son, Jesus Christ, to tell us that we have the power to live after the manner of happiness, and further, that we have the power within us to make the changes and do the things that make happiness possible in our lives.

Happiness is related to righteousness. The gospel plan is based upon living according to the eternal principles that govern heaven and earth. They are righteous principles. If we are a righteous people we may experience limitless happiness. I marvel that the Lord is so patient with us. He teaches us, loves us, and encourages us to trust in him and live after a pattern of his life, which is righteous living with a glad heart and faith in the goodness that such living can and will bring.

Living this way will greatly reduce the effects of the terrible, horrible, no good, very bad days that intrude themselves into our manner of living—of that I am very sure.

President George Albert Smith taught happiness when he said:

> It is a wonderful custom to wish one another happiness. Happiness is what we are all seeking, and it is what our Father in Heaven desires for us. Through the ages the Lord has inspired his prophets, and they have pointed the way of true happiness. (In Obert C. Tanner,

Christ's Ideals for Living [Salt Lake City, Deseret Sunday School Union Board, 1955], p. 283.)

The Prophet Joseph Smith said:

Happiness is the object and the design of our existence, and will be the end thereof, if we pursue the path that leads to it: and this path is virtue, uprightness, faithfulness, holiness, and keeping all of the commandments of God. (*Teachings of the Prophet Joseph Smith*, pp. 255-56.)

That same counsel is given by our beloved President Spencer W. Kimball today.

I was made sharply aware of the fact that we need to be happy when I saw a documentary film of a young Latter-day Saint family. The participants were working very hard at the tasks related to family life. They had achieved considerable efficiency in carrying out their responsibilities. But the camera didn't catch any joy or warmth or laughter that would indicate that they were a happy family.

I think happy interactions with each family member are very important. And I find myself anxious about that young couple and their children and about most of us because I am afraid that we are missing the very essence of life—the warmth and the joy of learning to live happily with each other.

There is no doubt that every day we will experience hardships and challenges, but with inspired prophets to direct us we can live a life of hope. Happiness is a possibility that can become a reality. It is fundamental to us—whether we are mothers of small children and have an intense desire to lead them in the paths of truth and righteousness, or if we are single women who haven't yet found an eternal companion, or if we are men and women suddenly alone after years of sweet companionship, or if we are students just embarking on years of higher education. Happiness is a tenet of our faith that should be kept ever before us.

As I talk to people and read daily events, I am convinced that we all need a massive dose of faith coupled with good cheer and righteous living. We need to help each other remember that we have the power within ourselves to be happy. I think I must have been given a large dose of this wonderful medicine of faith and happiness when I was a youngster. I truly believe it has inoculated me against many of life's tedious ills. I had a mother who believed that the way we looked at life made all the difference in the experiences that came to us. When there were hard tasks that needed to be done she would make up games to play with us and in that way we would complete our assignment and enjoy doing it. I remember one young man called to see me when we were bottling fruit. We had about five bushels of peaches left to put up. Mother couldn't spare me but she did invite him to join us if he wanted to. He did. He stayed and helped until every peach was put into the bottles and the clean-up was completed. Mother was a wonderful conversationalist with a remarkable sense of humor and so we talked and laughed as we worked. I don't believe any time we ever spent together was more fun.

Mother was not a Pollyanna who would pretend cheerfulness regardless of the circumstances. She had many hardships to endure. But she didn't burden us with them. She was against grumbling, whining, or complaining. She urged us to be mindful of our blessings and look for the positive things that life offered us.

I think mother shared the feelings of Donald Culross Peattie, who said, "Happiness comes of the grace to accept life gratefully and make the most of the best of it."

I would hope that each of us would learn this vital lesson and be grateful for life and live it as fully as possible.

In the book *The Hiding Place*, we read of Corrie Ten Boom, whose life teaches the importance of the application of Christian virtues. Such virtues prepared her for the hardships she experienced with the anti-Nazi underground activities.

As a teenager she willingly took over the task of keeping house. Her life would have been completely happy, she said, except for her concern about her Aunt Bep, who was slowly dying of tuberculosis. This situation was like a pall over the home—not the illness itself, for the aunt was lovingly cared for by her sister, but "her whole disgruntled and disappointed life."

Corrie's mother too was now more frequently in bed, and with a lot of pain. There she knitted caps and baby dresses or wrote encouraging letters for shut-ins. Oblivious of her own shut-in condition, she was cheerful and bright and expressed great sympathy for others confined to bed. Corrie, anxious about her aunt, spoke to her mother about it:

> "Can't we do something for Tante Bep? I mean, isn't it sad that she has to spend her last days here where she hates it, instead of where she was so happy? The Wallers' or someplace?"
>
> Mama laid down her pen and looked at me. "Corrie," she said at last, "Bep has been just as happy here with us—no more and no less—than she was anywhere else."
>
> I stared at her, not understanding.
>
> "Do you know when she started praising the Wallers so highly?" Mama went on. "The day she left them. As long as she was there, she had nothing but complaints. The Wallers couldn't compare with the Van Hooks where she'd been before. But at the Van Hooks she'd actually been miserable. Happiness isn't something that depends on our surroundings, Corrie. It's something we make inside ourselves." (*The Hiding Place*, pp. 18-19.)

Happiness begins first with faith, which is the fundamental force to set positive things in motion and make accomplishments possible. One needs faith in order to live in any realm of mortality beyond mere existence. For example, if you want to speak and understand a people that have a culture different from your own, you must have the faith that you can learn their ways and then find ways to do it, as missionaries do.

The scientist, when he begins to advance a hypothesis and then attempts to prove his reasoning, needs faith. Nor would a poet fashion the insightful phrase unless he or she had faith. So do you need faith every day of your life if you are to make a choice and decide how to approach each event. When your choices are based upon faith the day will be more satisfying.

Now, if in addition you choose to have faith in the divinely revealed truths, you will have even a further sense of purpose and direction in that decision that might not be made clear to you otherwise. You will find yourself enriched by a sense of harmony with all truth. You will find within you the promptings of the still, small voice directing, "Be of good cheer, little children; for I am in your midst, and I have not forsaken you" (D&C 61:36).

Think back to your childhood; remember when the fears of darkness were dispelled if your mother held you close and rocked you or when she tucked the blankets tightly around you when you had a bad dream. Or perhaps you climbed too far upon a sandstone butte and the only way down was to jump into the arms of your father, who called, "Come on, I'll catch you." You trusted him and he did catch you and you were safe. Your faith in your mother and father gave you security and well-being.

Faith in him, our all wise Heavenly Father, is the foundation stone of happiness for each of us.

Second, happiness comes from knowing that you, and only you, can make changes in your life. The Book of Mormon clearly states that "They have become free forever . . . to act for themselves and not to be acted upon" (2 Nephi 2:26).

The realization of this truth should free you from ever thinking that you are the victim of circumstances—rich or poor, whole or lame, male or female, old or young. I'm not suggesting that righteous living will free you from all of the problems and difficulties of life or that you are going to be given only ideal conditions in which to live. That is not the promise. The promise is that you have the power within you to act for youself. As long as you have the power to act for yourself there is much that you can do about the life you live. Think of the wonderful challenge that is yours to change some circumstance of your life that makes it difficult—or at other times to adjust your way of looking at life, as did Corrie Ten Boom's mother, so that you bring the richness of mortal experiences to every day.

Most important, it means that you will have the fundamental control over your happiness, because you have the power with which to change and adjust your life when you know the truth—that same truth which causes us to send our sons and daughters into the mission field to teach. Acceptance of gospel truths means making changes in our living to bring what we do into conformity with the eternal principles we believe. This practice can bring great and meaningful changes into our lives. Happiness isn't something that depends upon surroundings; happiness is something possible within yourself.

Third, happiness is to be found in doing those things that Jesus did when he walked upon the earth. It seems so natural for some to do. It may not always be easy.

French comedian Maurice Chevalier was asked how he always managed to be so cheerful. He said: "I don't always feel that way but when I sense an audience responding to the gaiety I am trying to give out, I feel gaiety coming back to me. It is like a boomerang —a blessed boomerang." (William Nichols, comp., *Words to Live By* [New York: Simon & Schuster, 1959], p. 29.)

I suppose no one knows that more than Relief Society sisters. A presidency in Southern California took me to see a sister who has multiple sclerosis. Those women have been helping her for years: cleaning her home, bathing her, fixing meals, and taking her to meetings. They said the more they did for her, the more happiness came back into their own lives. They found that, as Robert G. Ingersoll put it, "happiness is not a reward; it is a consequence."

I would hope that the consequence of your experience will help you find the real pleasure of doing good—revelling in the beauty of a flower you give to a neighbor as you say, "Thank you for just being you." There are so many things that you can do. There is not just one place to begin. I became even more aware of that fact when I read again the words of Robert Louis Stevenson:

> If I have faltered more or less
> In my great task of happiness;
> If I have moved among my race
> And shown no glorious morning face:
> If beams from happy human eyes
> Have moved me not; if morning skies,
> Books, and my food, and summer rain
> Knocked on my sullen heart in vain:
> Lord, thy most pointed pleasure take
> And stab my spirit broad awake.
> (James Dalton Morrison, ed., *Masterpieces of Religious Verse* [New York: Harper and Row, 1948] pp. 359-360.)

A "glorious morning face"? What is it? Have you ever seen one? Have you had one? A glorious morning face to me would be one that exhibits real pleasure and great anticipation.

Years ago when I was double dating one New Year's Eve the other girl had fallen asleep. When she awoke she was wreathed in smiles, and I felt a wonderful glow about her. I asked if she always awakened with such happiness. And she said, "Yes. I love to wake up. There is always great anticipation in it for me."

You've seen a glorious morning face, haven't you, when the weather is just perfect for that long-awaited ski trip? Or has it happened to you as you walked amid a profusion of wild flowers on a winding mountain trail? Or was it when you were given a gift made just for you with the hope that it would make you completely happy?

"The happiness of life is made up of minute fractions—the little soon forgotten charities of a kiss or smile, a kind look, a heartfelt compliment, and the countless infinitesimals of pleasurable and genial feelings," wrote Samuel Taylor Coleridge.

How many compliments, smiles, and charities have you given away today, this week, this month? They don't require money, but they might take a bit of extra loving and caring and some thought and time.

After a busy day of car-pool driving for a group of teenagers, one thirteen-year-old son said, "Mom, I want you to know how much I appreciate your driving me and my friends today. I know there are lots of other things you would rather be doing but you are here and I think you are great."

That mother had tear-dimmed eyes as she responded, "You'll never know how much that means to me today. It has been really hard to fit everything into place and I didn't think anyone cared."

Most of us live all of our lives just hoping for such a compliment because we want so very much to be assured that our work is of value to someone.

I heard Ardeth Kapp, general president of the Young Women of The Church of Jesus Christ of Latter-day Saints, tell a story I can't resist sharing with you. It was about a little boy who asked if he could go out and play for a couple of hours. His mother explained that he could go out but only for one half an hour because dinner was nearly ready and she wanted him to have it while it was piping hot. "Okay," he said as he left. "I'll just go out for a half an hour and I'll try not to have any fun." "Why not have fun for the half hour?" asked his mother. To which he replied, "Because time goes too fast when I'm having fun."

Have your full share of fun, but do it by loving and caring about people. Consider the many ways you can lift those around you. Be careful not to say the thoughtless word that can cause an injury or a hurt. Words can often be longer lasting than physical harm, even impede another individual in his or her growth, and stop your own progress toward righteous living.

One of California's well-known producers happened upon that truth during one of his frequent trips to New York City. He had decided that all New York cab drivers were impatient, bad-tempered, or hated their jobs, until he read the words of William Makepeace Thackeray: "The world is a looking glass and gives back to every man the reflection of his own face."

The next time he was in New York he thought upon those words and wondered if his bad experiences there could possibly be the result of his own thinking and outlook. So he decided to try a little experiment. He was cheerful, warm, and friendly and something very remarkable happened. He didn't meet one unpleasant taxi driver. He knew something had changed and felt it wasn't likely to be the cab drivers. He concluded, "To abandon making excuses for one's own shortcoming is like journeying to a distant land where everything is new and strange and very exciting."

Fourth, I would like to encourage you to experience happiness through kindness—and to expand your happiness past the smile and pleasant words to the great kindness exemplified in Fourth Nephi, where we are told that the people

> were in one, the children of Christ, and heirs to the kingdom of God. And how blessed were they! (4 Nephi 1:17.)
>
> They did walk after the commandments which they had received from their Lord and their God, continuing in fasting and prayer.

And there were no envyings, no strifes, nor tumults, nor whore-
doms, nor lyings, nor murders, nor any manner of lasciviousness;
. . . (4 Nephi 1:12, 16.)

Can you almost hear President Kimball's much-loved voice
explaining to you that when prayers are answered we are the ones
Jesus sends to do his errands? In that way the world is twice
blessed: blessed when the one who pleads to the Lord to hear and
give answer is served, and blessed when the one who gives the
service compassionately learns to meet another's need, thereby
bringing to the world the irrefutable evidence of the goodness
that exists among men when they live according to the word of
God.

When you believe in this way, you can help the blind to see by
detailing, as best you can, the beauty of the double rainbow that
arches across the sky. You can help heal the sick by picking up a
prescription, and preparing a cup of hot soup, or even by hand
carrying a heavy package. I know one lame girl whom a student
helped to walk. After she had undergone surgery to straighten her
feet, some students helped her walk over icy spots on the side-
walks; others even let her hold tight to their arms and took her
right to the classroom door. Could you also learn to sign if there
is a deaf neighbor who can't communicate with you otherwise? If
you do, miracles will begin to happen through your good works
and happiness will result.

We will reap that which we sow, as did Scrooge in Dickens's
Christmas Carol. He got only ridicule and denigration until he
changed and began to do kind deeds. In the process of giving of
himself, Scrooge became a new man such as had scarcely been
seen in all of England.

Five, be appreciative. We cannot find true happiness without
having a genuinely grateful heart. A grateful heart opens our
minds and souls to things around us as we begin to look for every
good thing.

The poet Robert E. Farley describes it this way:

> Think of the things that make you happy,
> not the things that make you sad;

Think of the fine and true in mankind,
    not its sordid side or bad;
Think of the blessings that surround you,
    not the ones that are denied;
Think of the virtues of your friendships;
    not the weak and faulty side.
(From the poem "Thinking Happiness,"
Peggy Howell, comp., *Joyous Journey* [Nash-
ville: Thomas Nelson, Inc., 1978], p. 47.)

Think of the things that make you happy. I asked my daughter
to tell me what made her happy and she said, "I'm happy when I
get a good night's sleep. I'm happy when I'm surrounded by
beauty: a clean house, contented children, and when I'm spending time with my husband and with my extended family." What
are the things that make you happy? Is it a date? An *A*? Is it the
glisten of the new-fallen snow undisturbed by humanity—or do
you like to see the deer tracks and footprints of people in the
snow that evidence life? What are the things that make you
happy?

Think of the fine and true in mankind. I remember President
N. Eldon Tanner telling me that he wanted each person that left
his office to leave feeling encouraged. That great man found the
fine and true in all mankind. His awareness of each person made
a difference in the way they responded to him. I know his
thoughtful ways made me happy. For example, do you think of
the virtues of your friendships, not the cruel and hostile words?

A would-be poet once referred to purple shadows and his
friend scoffed at him for using such an untrue, far-out description. "Whoever heard of purple shadows?" he ridiculed until he
felt confident he had taught his friend to be more credible in his
use of words. One day the friend saw something he had never
noticed before: purple shadows in the snow. If you were that
friend, could you make amends? If you were the poet, could you
think of the virtues of your friend and not of his cruel and hostile
word? It most often takes time and patient understanding to
develop lasting friendships. I hope the poet did not give up on his
friend.

Think of the hopes that lie before you. Think of the treasures you have gathered, and realize that you live at a time when you have the opportunity to glimpse the planets and get to know the earth and the skies as you have never known them before—if you are willing to take advantage of the disciplined study that your professors will prescribe for you. Can you sit still and listen while the musicians pour forth their deep emotions in measured sound? Have you learned to listen to the playwrights' view of a problem? My student granddaughter cannot believe that she will ever need to know the logarithm of 35 or how to graph a parabola, but these things will give her a better understanding of truth and someday she will be grateful for the focus and the perspective they bring to the experiences of her life.

Think of the service you may render, not of serving self alone; think of the happiness of others and in this you'll find your own!

Thinking happiness will help you learn to thank God each day for the wonders of life and its many opportunities, for the sheer joy of opening your mind to new ideas and searching for the harmony between the new insights and the iron rod that anchors your faith.

Stand still and listen to the still small voice and then breathe a prayer of thanksgiving for the comfort of knowing that God lives and that happiness comes from such schooling of the heart and the mind.

In the process of appreciating what you have, in savoring each new impression and sensory experience of sound or taste or touch you will enjoy a real taste of happiness. It is very important that we respond to people and all of the stimuli available in our daily activities. We cannot afford to let other people's efforts to make contact with us slide off from our unwilling hearts. We need to be awake and respond to every good overture. We cannot afford to be unresponsive or unappreciative.

Sixth, look for the good.

Grandma Moses was celebrated for her contributions in the world of art. In her book *My Life's History*, she writes a brief account of one year: "Then Anna was born, so I had four babies to care for. But we got along very nice till the children got the scarlet fever, that was a hard year but it passed on like all the rest. (In *Words to Live By,* William Nichols, comp. [New York: Simon and Schuster, 1959], p. 55.)

Those who knew her observed that Grandma Moses was articulate. Even in her later years of life she could describe many details about her wedding dress, a Thanksgiving dinner, and other things from her girlhood, but about a hard year she mostly remembered that it passed.

Make beauty, love, and laughter imperishable memories. Let the hardships pass. Lift others to loftier heights by looking for the good around you. Focus on the good things people do for you. Look for the beauty in the world; beauty is as much a reality as ugliness. Television offers a wide range of experiences but we can control it and our attitude regarding what is presented.

A photographer was given the responsibility of photographing the subway. He was afraid of the New York subway because at one time he had been mugged and his camera gear stolen. But he went back again and began to really look at the subway. Eventually he finished his book, and it had some of the ugly graffiti and the dark, dishevelled look of the New York subway, but his sensitive eye also caught the warmth of light and life that is to be seen there where human beings are. He had to learn to look for and savor those moments.

Look to goodness for the truth. *Search* for the truth. This life is to lead you to our Heavenly Father by keeping his commandments.

Bad days will come to all of us. Don't let your life on earth be filled with terrible, horrible, no good, very bad days; instead accept life gratefully and make the most of the best of it. You will then be prepared to live in a state of never-ending happiness because you have learned to live joyously in mortality.

As the song suggests, "In that bright morning, when [your] soul waketh and life's shadows flee," you will arise with the glorious thought, "I am with thee," and you will be filled with joy and gladness and rejoicing because the day of your deliverance will be at hand. Then your countenance will shine with radiance from being in the presence of the Lord. It will rest upon you and you will sing praises unto his holy name, because he gave you the opportunity in mortality to learn to live after a manner of happiness.

IV

Of the Great Work
of Love

15
Hearts So Similar

One November weekend, Heidi, a young Mormon mother in Salt Lake City, left her large and gracious home on a gray morning and drove over to Pioneer State Park and entered the restored home of Mary Fielding Smith.

Heidi was costumed in a dress reminiscent of one Mary might have worn, and for the entire day she welcomed young children from a nearby school into this small home, where she helped them learn to dry apples.

After the children left, the sun broke through the clouds overhead, illuminating not only the afternoon sky, but casting a reflective glow on the events of the day. That evening Heidi recorded in her journal, "I was overwhelmed by the exceptional beauty I could see from the little adobe house on the hill . . . I could hardly contain the light that streamed through the wavy glass window into my soul bringing feelings that were both very warm and very bright!"

She told about the contrast she felt between the small home in which she stood with its meager appointments and her own lovely house on another hill not far away. She wrote, "I hope my home is my family's place of strength, of faith, and of refuge, a place where truth is confirmed and testimony is strengthened, as Mary's little home had been for her family so long ago." She continued, "Despite life-styles so different, I was overcome by hearts so similar. My soul pleads to make the similarities count for my family, as they had for hers."

The circumstances of Mary Fielding Smith's life were much different from Heidi's.

In the momentous time of the exodus of the Saints from Nauvoo, Mary Fielding Smith found herself a widow with small children. To stay in Nauvoo would put her in the position of constant conflict with the dissidents and the mobs. To go would mean leaving her home unsold and, alone, shouldering the hardships and the unknown challenges of a long and wearisome trek by ox team.

To stay would mean giving up association with the Saints and the gospel she loved. This she could not and would not do. She wanted her children to grow up strong in the new and everlasting covenant.

The bonds of the gospel that led Mary Fielding Smith to face immense hardships and travel west with the Saints transcend time and trial, uniting sisters now as then in a oneness of faith.

From South America we received word of a woman who, when approached by missionaries to accept baptism, said, "You don't want me. I am nothing." But the missionaries persisted. She accepted the gospel, and it brought hope and love to her life; it brought learning and growth and progress. In time she became a Relief Society president, and through her devoted concern she could give that same hope and love to others.

One of the great sisters of Japan, Toshiko, wrote:

> Deep inside I had a feeling, I had a hope that there is a true chuch somewhere that testifies the resurrection of Jesus Christ . . . the Lord answered me . . . missionaries made a visit and I came to know the Book of Mormon . . . here in this teaching exists the truth I have been looking for . . . my heart had affinity for the gospel as desert sands have for water.

From Africa, where the first all-black Relief Society was founded in 1978, comes this word: "I have learned to look at life in a very different way. I, as a young mother, have learned how to bring up my children in a Christlike way. I have learned to make my home a pleasant place and also a place where the gospel is believed and lived.''

Example after example comes from women in many places, from women of greatly differing circumstances in life—women alone, women with children, women old, women young, women new to the Church, women in sorrow, women in despair, women happy.

They form a mosaic of many lives with differing circumstances, with individual talents, and with gifts wonderfully varied. The details of each life are so numerous that we begin to see in them the great diversity among us, and with it great strength and enrichment.

From varied experiences comes one great unifying truth, echoing and re-echoing: ''I know God lives and loves me. His teachings make me strong and sustain my soul.''

This testimony gives us hearts so similar that, as Paul said, ''We, being many, are one . . . in Christ'' (Romans 12:5).

We are many, with differing gifts, yet having hearts so similar —hearts testifying of the Lord Jesus Christ, that his teachings are true, his way of life a way of truth, of love, of light.

An examination of the many individual lives of those who would be his disciples testifies that nothing about the gospel is designed to ''make reason stare,'' as Eliza R. Snow observed so many years ago. (*Hymns*, no. 139.) The gospel, correctly understood, embraces all that is virtuous, lovely, of good report, and praiseworthy. (See Article of Faith 13.) The gospel is heaven-sent. It is the light by which we find our way through darkness and difficult times. The light of truth discloses our eternal nature. If we work hard enough and long enough, and pray diligently enough, the excellence that is our divine potential is possible to each one of us.

The uniqueness of each human being is a condition of God's creation, even though the differences sometimes cause us to wonder. One beautiful Oriental sister came to the United States and for the first time in her life encountered blonde-haired, blue-eyed persons. The blue eyes seemed so unusual to her, she later confided, that although she now thinks them lovely, she had at first wondered if people could actually see out of them.

Color, culture, talents, tastes—diversities abound and through them come much of the fulness and beauty we experience in this life. To the sister from the Orient it was the color of eyes that seemed strange at first, but for all of us there are differences we can come to appreciate more fully. Learning to value variety in others, we can also see and appreciate our own uniqueness more clearly.

When we can respect not only the differences in others but also their accomplishments, we begin to experience some of the joy the Lord intended. There is so much more of happiness to be had when we can rejoice in another's successes and not just in our own.

Being happy in the achievements of brothers, sisters, and associates requires a feeling of security and the recognition of our own great potential. The gospel brings this kind of confidence within the reach of each one. When we are filled with love for the Lord, with all our hearts, souls, and minds, the result is that we can feel and understand and be secure in his love. We will keep his commandments. We do love our neighbor as ourselves. This is the way he planned it to be for us, coming together in love and faith, with hearts so similar.

How do we become of one heart? We become so:

1. By knowing that we are daughters of God.
2. By knowing and witnessing that he lives and that his great mission is to make it possible for us to attain not only salvation but also exaltation.
3. By diligently—one step at a time—working at the task of perfecting ourselves.
4. By praying often for personal guidance and for a caring heart, one that understands and is aware of others.
5. By seeking divine help in living the teachings and judging not. We cannot walk in another's path. We cannot know another's challenges, and so we should not judge.

6. By living positively and giving all that we have to extend the work of the Lord, for sharing the truth of the gospel with another is one of the greatest gifts we can give.
7. By obtaining understanding and the strength to be actively engaged in those good things which will make the world a better place for our having been here.
8. By paying the price of excellence in all we undertake to do.
9. By willingly accepting the concept of selflessness—and translating it into the actions of our times and seasons.

These are the things that make us of similar hearts as we take personal responsibility for our own lives, whatever the circumstances. These principles can be embraced by all—the poor and the rich, single and the married, the young women and grandmothers. There are no exceptions and no specifications about looks, or marital status, or opportunities, or responsibilities. There are no arbitrary limitations.

The Lord really cares about the feelings of love in our hearts and souls, about diligence in seeking wisdom. He wants us to love and to care and do as he did. He wants us to be righteous as he was. He wants us to develop the divine within us.

We can be good women, elect women, and even holy women. Though we are women of great diversity, we can be women of God bound together in a great sisterhood of faith and testimony. And, like Heidi, we can pray for strength and faith and the ability to make our homes places of refuge where the light of heaven—like the golden sunlight of that gray November day—will stream into our lives no matter where we are. We, being many, should be one in Christ, and have hearts so similar.

16
The Bond of Charity

Charity is a teaching of the Lord. He has said, "And above all things, clothe yourselves with the bond of charity, as with a mantle, which is the bond of perfectness and peace" (D&C 88:125).

Many sisters care for each other in acts of tender compassion, ever striving for the highest, noblest, strongest kind of love—the pure love of Christ. Charity, or the pure love of Christ, is not synonymous with good deeds or benevolence. But kind, thoughtful, loving acts are the means by which Jesus has directed us to express our love—both our love for him and our love for others. If we have the sustenance, we are to give to those who want. If we are thoughtful, warm, and caring to those who are sick, those who mourn, those who are fatherless, those we love, and those who despitefully use us, then we have charity, for we are moved to act with compassion.

In Spanish the word *charity* means "the love that never ceases to be." In Micronesia the word *love* translates into "the power to change lives." These tender nuances give us a better understanding of the pure love of Christ. As we serve with the single desire to nurture all life, we come to know what charity means.

This seemed to be a characteristic of Ruth whose feelings for Naomi are recorded in the Old Testament. Ruth was compassionate, even though the circumstances of her life were bitter. Bitter experiences come into the lives of all of us. Without the bitter, we cannot know the sweet. The prophet Lehi explained: "For it must needs be, that there is an opposition in all things. If not so, . . . righteousness could not be brought to pass, neither wickedness, neither holiness nor misery, neither good nor bad. Wherefore, all things must needs be a compound in one." (2 Nephi 2:11.)

Ruth knew this opposition. She was just a young woman when her husband died and left her alone without children. It was a bitter time, and yet, there was the sweetness of her relationship with her mother-in-law and the strength of her faith in the God of Israel. Both had come into her life because of her marriage.

Ruth gleaned from the fields to sustain herself and Naomi. But greater than what she gleaned from the fields were the experiences that came as she worked to thresh out the wheat from the chaff. At the end of her day, she had great blessings because of her effort. This is the challenge we all face in our own lives. We too must glean from life's circumstances and experiences that which will give us growth and faith and peace of mind.

There is no way that we can, or should want to, escape the challenges and struggles of mortality. How we struggle with them is our choice. The gospel plan gives us an eternal perspective that should help us have courage to be about our gleaning.

As his daughters, we should walk step by step toward perfection. Relief Society can be a guide, a strength, a light, a direction. Relief Society can teach us how to develop a love that never ceases. It provides an opportunity to demonstrate love by our actions. Relief Society will help us sort out the truth from error in a modern world, in what Lehi called a compound of good and evil.

Eight directives are crucial if we are to develop the bond of charity.

1. Learn, then teach. Recall when Jesus sat at the table with his disciples just before his suffering in Gethsemane. He reminded them that "he that is greatest among you, let him be . . . as he that doth serve" (Luke 22:26). He turned to Simon and said, "Simon, Simon . . . I have prayed for thee, that thy faith fail not: and when thou art converted, strengthen thy brethren" (Luke 22:31-32).

The procedure that the Lord revealed to Simon Peter is given to us all. We must know the principles of truth and then go forth converted and teach those principles to others.

Determine to teach—learn through lessons prepared by inspiration, learn upon your knees in humble prayer, learn by studying the scriptures, learn by listening to the modern prophets, learn by listening to the promptings of the Holy Ghost. And when you have learned, teach—strengthen your children, your husband, your associates. Teach them through each opportunity that comes to you; teach them by the life that you live.

2. *Be active in Relief Society.* To be active in the Relief Society a woman needs to attend the meetings of Relief Society and accept assignments. Whether you are old or young, married or single, attend Relief Society and develop a bond of sisterhood with other women who share your concerns and beliefs. Be there. Participate in the lesson discussions.

One day as I turned to leave President Spencer W. Kimball's office, I asked, "Is there anything I can do for you?" "Yes," he replied, "you can get the women to Relief Society."

I believe he asked me to address that problem because he knows that attendance at Relief Society provides us opportunities to be spiritually strengthened, to enlarge our understanding of eternal truths, and thus it helps us make choices in our lives that will allow us to save ourselves. If your present callings take you to Primary or to the Young Women's meetings, reach out for other ways to become close to your Relief Society sisters. Read the lessons. Discuss them with your visiting teachers. Make Relief Society a part of your life.

3. *Spread the gospel message.* When Joseph Smith addressed the Saints for the last time in the dusty streets of Nauvoo en route to Carthage, he reminded them that their work was to minister life

and salvation to all the world. President Kimball continues to remind us that it is our great responsibility to lengthen our stride and preach the gospel to all the nations.

As women of the Church we need to prepare to do missionary work by study, by prayer, and by service. Then we will be better able to live by the principles of truth, and others seeing our "good works" are more apt to be accepting. The greatest numbers of baptisms come from among those people who know active Latter-day Saints.

Even as our sons and daughters go out every year to bring to thousands the message of salvation, our local Relief Society units can find many ways that Relief Society women may cooperate with the full-time missionaries of the Church to bring the good tidings to other thousands. An important beginning is to give the missionaries nonmembers' names so they can teach regularly.

Consider the possibility of a mission for yourself, either as a proselyting missionary or as a special services missionary.

Be genuinely interested in getting to know people in community service, in your neighborhood, in the work place—wherever your day's activities take you. Be honest in your friendship and sincere in living what you believe, and then your opportunities for sharing the gospel will develop.

4. *Learn and live the principles of welfare work.* Remember that the essence of the gospel plan is caring for the poor and the needy, developing a provident home, and contributing so that there will be commodities to meet the needs of those who must call upon them. Everyone has the God-given challenge to extend love and compassion to those who have special needs and are heavily burdened.

5. *Be sensitive to life's transitions, both for yourself and for others.* Be constantly aware of the realities of life, which include many transitional phases—from youth to maturity, from single to married, from a house filled with children to an empty house, from military to civilian life, from employment to retirement, from married to widowed or divorced, from young and vibrant to old and dependent. Each transition brings with it a special set of

stresses and concerns. Each of us needs a listening ear at times, and encouragement as we seek to find our way. We must be sensitive to the changes that come into each other's lives.

6. *Do quality visiting teaching.* Visiting teaching is a tool given to us by the Lord. Properly used, it is a great source of inspiration, strength, and comfort. Many a sister's prayers have been miraculously answered by visiting teachers in a time of need. In an urban world that is often filled with loneliness in the midst of a crowd, visiting teachers are essential. They are the Lord's way of keeping his daughters in touch with each other, and I think they are his recognition of the sanctity of each home. What the visiting teaching program needs is for us to have more dedication to those we are called to visit.

7. *Be a connecting link.* Look at yourself as a connecting link between the past and the future. Individually you already are a link in the great ongoing human experience. But you can also shape an understanding of our times by the journals you leave, and by the things you choose to value and keep. Be a vital part of linking together for eternity those who went before you, those who live now, and those who are yet to come.

8. *Value yourself.* The scriptures bear witness that our Heavenly Father values his children above all of his other creations. In his children are to be found immortality and eternal life. Each of us has the potential to become as he is.

Each woman in the Church should realize that none of the blessings which our Father has for his faithful daughters will be denied any who live worthily.

Let us unite and become one sisterhood. Together we can become instruments in the hands of God by which he can perform his work. We will be motivated to good works by the accepting, encouraging, enobling love of Christ.

17

The Relief Society in Times of Transition

Recently my husband and I returned to our home on a hill over-looking the Salt Lake Valley to find that all of the electrical power was off in our neighborhood. As we approached our darkened house, a young neighbor boy observed us returning home in the darkness and ran over to offer his lantern. "We have another one at our house," he said. "You can keep this one as long as you need it."

I was impressed by the concern of that little boy. He had a light he was willing to share. He really cared about us. He was prepared to help us in our time of need.

I thought a great deal about that little boy in the days that followed. He was so helpful, so happy, and so willing to share his light.

To me, his actions represent the fundamental message of the gospel of Jesus Christ and the motto of Relief Society as well: "Charity never faileth." My young friend was prepared. He and his family had a light on hand to help them pierce the darkness when their primary source of light was temporarily withdrawn.

We each should take seriously the counsel to prepare. Recall the parable of the ten virgins, in which they "took their lamps, and went forth to meet the bridegroom. And five of them were wise, and five were foolish. They that were foolish took their lamps, and took no oil with them: But the wise took oil in their vessels with their lamps.'' When the bridegroom came, they were ready. They "went in with him to the marriage: and the door was shut.'' (Matthew 25:1-10.)

We should have the wisdom to personally prepare by understanding truth and living it with integrity so that we might be worthy disciples of Christ. Then, with him as the center of our lives, we can develop those Christlike qualities which will make us worthy of exaltation. We will gain added strength and a greater capacity for love. We will improve the skills of giving our love in such a way that we are prepared in the time of need.

My young friend also cared enough to observe a need. He ran to us in the darkness. He held out his light to illuminate our darkened way.

Jesus directs us to do that in poignant parables, saying: "For I was an hungred, and ye gave me meat: I was thirsty, and ye gave me drink: I was a stranger, and ye took me in: Naked, and ye clothed me: I was sick, and ye visited me: I was in prison, and ye came unto me.'' (Matthew 25:35-36.)

He clearly explains that we must care enough to offer ourselves to meet the physical and spiritual needs of those around us. Doing this is charity. It is a beginning of the pure love of Christ.

I listened to a young mother address a ward Relief Society meeting. She told us that she was losing her eyesight. She expressed gratitude for those who had been reading to her, driving her to appointments, and for another sister who was teaching her to play the piano. Relief Society sisters through their acts of kindness had offered her their light and helped to lessen the fear of this very difficult time of her transition into a world of darkness.

Dislocating, often anguishing transitions are something we all face. They will be different for each of us. Serious illness or permanent malady is but one. Others may be the death of a loved one, a child or a husband; the realization that one may never marry in this life; divorce; returning home from a mission; a marriage without children; marriage of the last child; the change from high school to college; a move to a new location; and on and on.

Each of these circumstances necessitates a particular mode of adaptation and requires the development of new and different ways to adjust to an altered life-style that may be challenging or painful. It is the very nature of such turning points that makes old patterns of behavior no longer adequate or appropriate.

We should constantly prepare ourselves to meet new challenges and to helpfully, willingly, and happily reach out to others in their time of need. The Relief Society should be a light for sisters in times of transition. Officers and teachers and members should systematically concern themselves with the stresses and the distresses of transition that our sisters face.

A recently widowed woman, who has always gained satisfaction from doing for others, found it very difficult to ask for help. She wisely made herself do it because she said it may prove helpful to someone else. She also had enough faith to know that she could do for someone else when she was self-sufficient again.

A young woman, released from the highly disciplined structure of a mission, is still motivated to convert the world. But, as she said, "I must learn to face reality and set priorities in this new environment, even though I feel uncomfortable in activities such as dating or swimming or even just reading a novel."

A woman at a singles conference shared with me the terrible reality of her recent divorce after twenty years of marriage. "You cannot know the courage it is taking for me just to walk into that room filled with single people, knowing that I am one of them now. I cannot even begin to describe how hard it is," she said.

Can we really appreciate what another suffers? Probably not, but we have learned some important things about hard transitions that may help us to better understand ourselves or someone else in those difficult periods of change:

1. A transition may prove an opportunity for spiritual, physical, intellectual, and psychological development—or it can become a time of serious deterioration. The way is new and often difficult. It takes a great deal of courage and

sometimes support from others to make a transition a time of growth.

2. In a time of transition, it is less the traumas of childhood that shape our ability to adjust to the change. It is more often the quality of sustained relationships with other people that makes the difference. Positive, supportive, ongoing relationships are a valuable resource in times of major changes in one's life.

3. It is not the transition itself that is of primary importance in seeking adjustment, but rather how the transition fits an individual's circumstance at the time it occurs. Each person's adjustment will be different because people are different, even though the crisis may seem to be the same.

4. There is often a measure of disorganization in a time of transition, but adaptation is more rapid and secure when there is reliable support from friends and associates.

Can you begin to realize how important the sisterhood of Relief Society is? Secure friendships and faith can make good transitions possible. Both were there as the widow asked for help, as the divorced woman received courage, as the returned missionary adjusted to her new life-style, as the young mother adapted to her encroaching blindness.

As we begin to understand the countless transitions that can affect our lives, we also come to know that transitions can both intensify and increase with the changes in our complex society.

We fill the place of family for many women—to be part of that reliable circle of ongoing friendships that are so necessary to provide support when a woman's own strength is inadequate and wanting.

We can heighten our sensitivity to our neighbor's needs, increasing our capacity to serve. And perhaps we may need to draw back a bit from other preoccupations that may not be as worthy of our time.

We can develop attitudes of love and caring by remembering our basic Christian commitment to forgiveness, gentleness, and kindness. We can promote the goodwill among people that heralded the birth of the Savior, and we can encourage a profound personal appeal to our Heavenly Father for peace and strength to face adversity.

But even immense goodwill cannot help us reach out to all sisters, making certain that none is overlooked. We must have a program, and we do. The Relief Society is designed for this very purpose. During one of the first meetings of the Nauvoo Relief Society, Lucy Mack Smith stated: "This institution is a good one. . . . We must cherish one another, watch over one another, comfort one another, and gain instruction." (Minutes of the Female Relief Society of Nauvoo, March 17, 1842; in *History of Relief Society 1842-1966,* [Relief Society General Board 1966], p. 20.)

The Relief Society program can help us reach even the needs we may not know exist. I was told about one visiting teacher who, in a caring attitude, sent the sisters she visits a Christmas card. When she went to preparation meeting, the message teacher asked the visiting teachers to send a Christmas card to each of the sisters they visit and include their personal note with the card.

The visiting teacher was perplexed. She had already sent the cards, but she did not write the personal note. After debating with herself for some time she finally determined to send another card, this one with a personal note.

When she visited her assigned sisters in January, she went first to the home of an inactive member. When she entered the room, she could see that all evidences of Christmas had been put away —except for one card standing alone on a small table. It was the card with the note in it. The sister explained that she had left the card out to show her nonmember friends that members of her church go the second mile. She said that she had told them this before, but now she had some tangible evidence they could see.

When the visiting teacher went back the next month, the house was tidy, the furniture dusted, and the card still stood on the small table. The next month, the card was still there—and the next, and the next.

The visiting teacher had not realized that this inactive sister needed a positive manifestation of concern. She also learned how much even small acts of kindness do matter.

By filling a Relief Society calling, a sister can increase her understanding of others. She can learn how to care, perhaps while she is helping another make that difficult transition from inactivity to full participation. Every position in Relief Society should help a sister not only to serve, but to grow—to progress toward the goals that she has set for her life, to strengthen herself, her family, and her social relationships as she develops the attributes of godliness. Every lesson attended in Relief Society should help her understand a principle of the gospel—what it is, how it can find expression in her life, and how she is better able to serve others because of it.

A homemaking miniclass must go beyond merely teaching the techniques of a skill. It must engender attitudes of selfless giving with which the skill can be gladly employed.

A major concern of the Relief Society today is to reach out to each young woman as she assumes the vital work of her life and to help her understand the limitless opportunities of a woman in the Church. Do not underestimate the young Relief Society sisters, their capacity, their ability, their desire, and their willingness to share in the involvement of Relief Society responsibilities. Their physical maturity is often surpassed by their spiritual readiness and the vitality and freshness of their intellectual perceptions. Include them. Teach them. Learn from them.

And young Relief Society sisters, we know that Relief Society is stronger because of your contributions. Will you also let Relief Society help you learn to meet the challenges of adulthood with greater confidence and vision?

Forget not the transition of old age. Statistics point out that an ever larger number of women will be widowed. Most women will live to an age that would have seemed extraordinary a generation ago. The aging process can be a graceful time of fulfillment, or it can be a time of frustration.

My heart ached as I was told of a ward Relief Society president who called the daughter of an aging member of her Relief Society and said, "Your mother has given long years of service in our ward. But she is old now, and if you want her to attend the meetings and the socials, you must assume the responsibility to bring her. We will not do it."

Relief Society's response to aging sisters like her must take into account the physical impairment that often accompanies old age, and must determine how to be helpful. We should be happy and willing to assist our older sisters. Their loneliness can be as debilitating as disease, and their isolation a prison from which there seems to be no escape. For many, their constant companion is a feeling of worthlessness or inconvenience. We have the responsibility to include them, and the greater opportunity to learn from them.

Relief Society has a practical communication network to ensure that no sister, young or old, is neglected or forgotten. Visiting teachers, I plead that you take the spirit of Relief Society into each home. Care for the lonely. Be at the bedside of the ailing. Share the light of the gospel in a world of much gloom.

James Thomson observed: "Light! nature's resplendent robe; without whose vesting beauty all were wrapt in gloom."

Help dispel gloom. Bring the light of truth. Do it through your senses, through your reason, and most significantly through the Spirit. It does not matter who you are or what you are currently doing with your life. The light of truth is there waiting to be discovered, and, being discovered, waiting to illuminate the life of each child of God.

In times of transition and often great upheaval, it is easier for individuals to become paralyzed by the gloom than to have the illumination of the Spirit. That is why they need us to search for them and share the gospel light. This should become a resolve in the heart of each sister.

In the play *Winterset*, Mio says, "I came here seeking light in darkness, running from the dawn, and stumbled on a morning." Prepare to give of your light, even in the darkness of your own nights, so that you too will stumble onto a beautiful morning.

Alma suggests that committed Church members are willing to "bear one another's burdens, that they may be light; Yea, and are willing to mourn with those that mourn; yea, and comfort those that stand in need of comfort, and to stand as witnesses of God at all times and in all things, and in all places." (Mosiah 18:8-9.) This passage beautifully portrays the role women in the Church should assume to help one another through periods of transition, for it speaks of commitment to compassionate giving, to sympathetic understanding, and to encompassing concern.

Let your light shine out and your love reach out until you find yourselves illuminated and warmed by a charity that never faileth.

V

Of Loving and Living in the World

18
Women for the Latter Day

It was in 1874 that Eliza R. Snow said, "Paul the apostle anciently spoke of holy women. It is the duty of each one of us to be a holy woman. We shall have elevated aims, if we are holy women. We shall feel that we are called to perform important duties. No one is exempt from them. There is no sister so isolated, and her sphere so narrow but what she can do a great deal towards establishing the Kingdom of God upon the earth." (*Woman's Exponent*, September 15, 1873, p. 62.)

The method outlined by the Lord is to learn line upon line, precept upon precept. Set realistic, achievable goals so that you can feel the joy of a victory over yourself. And then give of what you have learned to help others.

I have a friend with a large family of twelve children. Although she has days of discouragement, generally speaking she makes progress by having a prepared routine each morning to get ready for the day. This is her four-point plan: One, she gets out of bed early to exercise. She hates to exercise so she hurries to get it out of the way. Two, she reads the scriptures. She enjoys that so much she has to make herself stop at her determined one-half hour. Three, she prays, sharing her gratitude and her concerns, and in this way she feels the Lord's guidance and direction even when things don't work out the way she had planned. Four, she has a positive, happy attitude as she greets her children. It was the only way, she said, that she could feel she was growing.

I wish all of us could attend to our home responsibilities with the vision of my friend. She certainly hasn't obtained perfection there, but she has learned the importance of loving her husband and their children, showing it in laughing with them. She may not know that C. S. Lewis has wisely said of homemakers, "it is surely in reality the most important work in the world. What do ships, railways, mines, cars, and governments etc. exist for except that people may be fed, warmed, and safe in their own homes? . . . We wage war in order to have peace, we work in order to have leisure, we produce food in order to eat it. So your job is the one for which all others exist." (*Letters to C.S. Lewis*, Warren H. Lewis, ed., [London: Geoffrey Bles Ltd., 1956], p. 62.)

Any woman who understands the purpose of life, who gives her time and energy to make a loving home, and dedicates herself to helping her husband and children grow and become their best selves, is a "holy woman."

I believe my daughter and her husband caught some of that vision of building the kingdom when they decided to dedicate themselves to teaching and training their children in some eternal truths. As a counselor in the bishopric, he had the opportunity to interview the children of the ward as they became candidates for baptism and he found that many of them had a hard time repeating the Articles of Faith. He conferred with my daughter and they determined to use part of each family home evening to work with their own children, then not old enough for baptism, and help them become acquainted with these great statements of our faith. He wanted to see if their little ones, the oldest only four, could learn the words. He wanted to see how difficult it would be. Together they entered upon this venture.

Before he was five their young son could repeat the Articles of Faith and he understood something of their meaning because his father and mother explained them to him. One night he struggled with the fourth Article of Faith until the time came for him to go to bed. The little boy protested, "But I haven't got the words yet." His mother lovingly said, "That's all right, we'll work on it tomorrow." But the child could not let it go and she found him struggling with the words every time she looked in upon him that night. By morning, however, he had mastered them and he came to her with great delight to say, "I've got them now, Mama."

Let me tell you what happened after this little boy mastered all the words of the thirteen Articles of Faith. His little friend, the daughter of an inactive mother and nonmember father, told her mother of Joshua's achievement and then said, "Mama, will you teach me the Articles of Faith at family home evening?" And her mother said, "Yes, I'll teach you."

I took Joshua with me when I was asked to speak at the Missionary Training Center and introduced him to the missionaries. I asked him to repeat the Articles of Faith for them. After that, in many places where I traveled missionaries would tell me that listening to this little boy say the Articles of Faith had helped them renew their own efforts to memorize the exact words. "If he could do it," they would say to me, "I knew I could too, so I tried again."

But the most significant result of the patient, loving teaching was the impact it has had upon Joshua. Knowing the words of the Articles of Faith, he could relate to more and more of what the speakers in Church were saying. He began to understand more and more about the teachings of the Church and of Jesus.

Any woman who patiently teaches and trains her little children about eternal truths is building the kingdom of God on earth.

A young girl sat next to her mother as she listened to her father deliver a major address. In the middle she turned to her mother and said, "Daddy's talk isn't going at all well!" Her mother whispered, "Don't criticize him, pray for him."

A child's ability to do is frequently made possible by a mother's faith in him or her. It is a "holy woman" who devotes herself to providing the sustaining love that helps another climb the mountains of discouragement and "not doing well."

A former temple president and matron presided over a mission. Two weeks after they returned home he had a stroke and was left practically immobile. His wife said, "The Lord has prepared us for this day by letting us know his plan. I will help make these years the happiest days of your life."

A woman who can come to the end of her life with so loving an attitude would be close to establishing a little of heaven on earth.

It is no accident that women are creating this "little bit of heaven" in so many places and under extraordinary stress. They are being trained and strengthened in their Relief Societies and through their own loving service in many callings.

Wherever I have gone throughout the Church I have been greeted by Relief Society presidents full of faith, sensitive to the circumstances of the sisters they serve, willing to help shoulder the burdens of those who suffer, eager to be at the work of the kingdom. They too are the "holy women" of whom Paul spoke.

I know one Relief Society president who has been my companion since childhood, my only sister, who, though older than I, has sustained me with love throughout my time in office as the general president. She, as a stake Relief Society president, was diligent in carrying out every assignment and her stake was the first to turn in their funds for the building of the Nauvoo monument to women. She and her stake board have helped the work of Relief Society move forward in countless ways. She is characteristic of the many who lead the women of the stakes of Zion.

The care with which the women of the Church prepare their lessons and their organized compassionate service invites the ratifying spirit of the Lord to be part of the studying and learning.

In my own ward I am made humble by the great efforts our sisters provide as they care for the little children in the Primary. I took my granddaughter into the meeting during her weekend stay at our home and the teacher welcomed her and introduced her lovingly to each child in the class as a new friend; soon her shyness evaporated and she was happily involved in the class. I went to my own Relief Society meeting and found myself royally filled by the excellence of the teacher's work.

These are women who feel a stewardship has been given them, and they are willing to do the work of the kingdom with excellence, that the influence of the gospel light might be felt wherever they are.

My heart was deeply touched by the obedience and courage of sisters I met in a country at war. I heard the branch Relief Society president commend them for their commitment to their home and families, to the work of the Lord, and to each other during the perilous times they faced each day. She said, "You never know when you step outside your door whether you will be attacked by terrorists, yet you do your visiting teaching and attend all of your church meetings. You are courageous women who do a mighty work in such a time as this."

We must fortify ourselves so that when hard or lonely moments come, we can call upon God for his strength, wisdom, and vision, that we might act according to righteous principles.

We can rejoice in being among those whom the Lord has sent to the kingdom to accomplish his work, to raise children unto him, to spread his gospel, to prepare a generation to greet him on his return.

May we all rise to the challenge of being holy women in these latter-days, that this "chosen generation . . . an holy nation . . . [might] shew forth the praises of him who hath called [us] out of darkness into his marvellous light." (1 Peter 2:9.)

19

For Such a Time as This

Life is a challenge, or one long series of them. With mid-terms and finals students are required to measure how well they are doing in their classes. In a very real sense, no one knows what has been learned without the test. A way of life can be designed to create Saints, but it is difficult to measure a person's progress until a situation arises that reveals the inner person. In a way it is like the test. C. S. Lewis gives an example of this kind of examination when he suggests that a crisis does not cause a person to be charitable or ill-tempered, it simply reveals the ill-tempered or charitable person he is. We are continually preparing and experiencing such tests, great or small, planned and unintended, as the circumstances of our lives develop and change.

In the account of Esther as we read it in the Bible, the young, lovely Esther had only recently been made queen, and the king, not aware that she was Jewish, had allowed a proclamation to be sent throughout the kingdom that on a particular day all the Jewish people should be killed. Mordecai, her uncle, realized that Esther might be able to save her people. He sent word for her to go before the king and plead with him to spare the Jews. This was difficult for Esther, who, although she was queen, did not have the right to go to the king unless he called for her.

If she were to go, and he refused to acknowledge her, she would be put to death. Yet she knew she was probably the only one in a position to help. It was a moment of great decision for young Queen Esther. She was being asked to risk her life for her people.

Mordecai helped her to see beyond her own peril to the opportunity she was being given when he counseled, "Who knoweth whether thou art come to the kingdom for such a time as this?" (Esther 4:14).

In one of the greatest demonstrations of courage found in the Old Testament, Esther did go, and she won the king's favor.

Confronting the king at the risk of her life did not make Esther courageous; rather, it revealed the courage that was within her—and not only the courage, but the compassion and the devotion to her people.

I am deeply touched by her response: "Go, gather together all the Jews that are present in Shushan, and fast ye for me, and neither eat nor drink three days, night or day: I also and my maidens will fast likewise; and so will I go" (Esther 4:16).

Few of us will have the opportunity to plead before a king. But all of us will sometime find out whether we can respond "greatly" when faced with an unexpected challenge.

We have no reason to believe that Esther had prepared specifically for the role she had to play, and yet all her life was preparation, as mine is and as yours is.

Preparation may be conscious and skillful or casual and undirected, but in either case, it is cumulative. As Richard L. Evans reminded us, "What is going to happen is happening." We may not realize it at the moment of choice, but our response is an infallible index of what we have become.

President David O. McKay when he was a young man loaded stock for market. There always seemed to be an admiring crowd of small boys looking on. The McKay brothers, unlike many of their neighbors, did not dress in overalls and heavy boots when they were working. By rural standards they were elegantly turned out as they loaded calves, sheep, and hogs into the waiting wagons with speed and grace. Nearing the end of their labor, young David O. decided he would hoist the last hog aboard all by himself. As he started the mighty heave it would take, he slipped and ended up with the hog on top of him, both of them deep in the loading corral mud. The boys sitting on and peering through the fence waited expectantly.

Slowly David extricated himself, wiped futilely at the muck that now almost covered him, and then said to the assembled youngsters, "No use waiting, boys, I'm not going to swear!"

His decision not to swear on this occasion was the same as it had been on many other occasions. The control of his tongue, in a moment of stress and humiliation, was reinforced by the countless other times when he had resisted the easy and insecure recourse of profanity.

We rarely succumb to temptation in one overpowering moment. The strength of living by a principle is built line upon line, time upon time of facing a moment of challenge and responding appropriately.

Every important choice is the inevitable result of a hundred earlier choices. And so it was that Esther, who had been reared in a home of faith and obedience, was prepared for her great test of courage. She not only determined to go into the king unbidden but was ready to accept the full consequence of her act, saying, "I will go into the king, which is not according to the law: and if I perish, I perish" (Esther 4:16).

I thought of Esther when I learned of a young soldier who, upon returning from Vietnam, bore his testimony. His job was to go ahead of his company as they moved into a new area of battle, checking the fields for mines and testing the enemy fire. He said, "Although I knew I might get shot in the head at any moment, I also knew that the next instant would be better than anything I had ever known."

The playwright Maxwell Anderson, in depicting young Joan of Arc, another who had lived so that she would respond magnificently to great challenges, expresses concepts that might apply to any young person who must consider giving up life for a righteous cause.

> Every man gives his life for what he believes. Every woman gives her life for what she believes. Sometimes people believe in little or nothing, nevertheless they give up their lives to that little or nothing. One life is all we have, and we live it as we believe in living it, and then it's gone. But to surrender what you are and live without belief —that's more terrible than dying—more terrible than dying young. (*Joan of Lorraine*, Act 5.)

Most lives, will not experience the dramatic either/or of live or die, but there will be many times when the question is whether one believes or does not believe. Most of us also will have the chance to learn the meaning of "Thy will, not mine, be done."

The story of Jonah can be instructive to us. Jonah was not quick to respond when the Lord asked him to go and preach against Nineveh. Only after his experience in the whale did he accept this call. Then, when the people of Nineveh unexpectedly repented, one and all (even their cattle wore sackcloth), and the Lord did not destroy them, Jonah was disappointed. He had promised destruction if they did not repent. He could not adjust to the idea that they had repented. He went off by himself, sat down, and pouted. (Jonah 4:1-3.)

He was experiencing what many now call cognitive dissonance—the inability to accept something that is in conflict with what you think it should be. Terry Warner's small child said it charmingly: "It's when you know what you want to do and what's right to do, and you get a fuss in your mind."

I think we have all experienced the frustration or the feeling of loss, verging on abandonment, when plans we have counted on seem to go very wrong. But to see someone who can accept deep disappointment and adjust or even triumph is profoundly moving. It is especially so for parents who would, on the one hand, wish to spare their children any sorrow or pain and, on the other, desire nothing more than to have them become strong and able to withstand trials.

Let me share with you the story of our high school basketball star—at least he was a star to me and to the beautiful blonde coed who as a pep club member always chose to decorate his room, make him treats, and letter him clever posters during the state tournaments. It didn't take too many of those experiences before they started to date. She loved to watch him play. She would keep the game statistics privately so that she could discuss them with him, encouraging him when he especially needed it and keeping him from becoming too proud if he had an exceptionally good night. Their casual, fun dating turned into a genuine courtship with marriage plans, in the future, because he had a mission to complete. Both of those things happened as they hoped they would. Then came their temple marriage. Many guests at their wedding reception would comment on the fact that they were a perfect couple. The bride was radiant and beautiful. The groom was considered handsome. Frequently I would hear, "I can't wait to see your children. They will be knockouts!"

They too dreamed and planned for the happy days when they would have lovely children, and they openly declared that they wanted to have a basketball team made up of their very own sons.

The day arrived when they were to welcome their firstborn child into the world. We went to the hospital to be with them. Each moment seemed so long and it was filled with excitement and anticipation and that constant hope that it would be the beginning of their basketball team. Their star was about to be born.

When they wheeled the mother out of the delivery room we asked expectantly, "Well, was it a boy or a girl?" "It's a boy!" said the proud new father and we rejoiced together. Then they uncovered the baby's legs and we saw that he had twisted, malformed feet.

Quickly his brave little mother said, "My mother said my foot was crooked when I was born; perhaps they will straighten themselves." But the doctors confirmed the fact that only surgery could give him normal use of his feet.

He had surgery. He wore casts, then braces. We laughed when a little neighbor boy said, "Why can't I wear shoes like Davy?" By the way, he was a "knockout." He had red hair and a sweet, happy disposition. He was given a name that connotes a special love, but the basketball dreams and plans of those two people were shattered. They had to begin anew to think about what they really wanted for him. That little boy was taught to walk and play and run. He can handle a ball about as well as any boy his age but he will never excel in basketball the way that they had dreamed.

An even more sobering challenge came to another friend, whose husband was one of the top ten medical students at Temple University. On the night before his graduation he fell and severely fractured his skull. He was in a coma for six weeks. After recovering he had many hard decisions to make, such as whether to continue his training for surgery or to become a dermatologist instead. He and his sweetheart carefully considered the extent of his injury and the demanding field he had chosen. It was decided that there would be less strain, and probably greater success, if he changed his specialty. Another difficult decision was whether to marry. He asked himself if he would be well enough and capable of caring for a wife and children. After hours and hours of discussion and planning they finally determined that perhaps, if he had plenty of rest and good care, he could continue to heal and he could assume the responsibilities of a husband and father. Other than the constant pain in his head, he led a somewhat normal life and had a good practice for thirteen years. Three children were born to him and his wife during that time, and then all their fears came to pass. The pain became more constant and more intense. He became so forgetful that he had to undergo surgery to remove the adhesions that filled his head. They were successfully treated but he contracted meningitis with accompanying high fever. He lost control of his body functions. His memory was irreparably damaged. His wife could no longer give him the complete care he needed at home. He would have to be hospitalized for as long as he lived. Brokenheartedly, she faced the reality that this special chapter of their lives together had to be closed. A new one was opening. It was one of faith and love and devotion and further adaptation.

For twenty-two years this courageous woman has worked to support herself and their children, but during this time through her determined effort she has made their father a very special part of their lives. She has taken their family activities to his hospital room as often as possible. Many times he couldn't even recall that the family had been there.

Many have said to the wife, "There isn't a court in the land that wouldn't give you a divorce."

She smiles and says, "At another time and in another place we want to be together honoring the commitments we have made to each other. He won't have the encumbrance of a broken body then, and we will be able to live abundantly and everlastingly together."

Making long-range plans brings us the pleasure that comes with expectation and progress that is the result of purpose. But other essential growth and even a more profound joy can often only come from adjusting our hopes to an altered plan.

It is important to be thinking ahead and determining our objectives. But although we need to have future goals clearly projected, we should not fail to appreciate possible alternatives and the reality of the present. Our objective is not more important than how we reach it. We might focus so totally upon a goal that we fail to realize that life is being spent on our way to achieving it. Santayana philosophized, "Life is what happens while we are planning for something else."

Someone has remarked that the trouble with life is that it is so daily. Our reactions to those day-by-day demands determine the stature of our lives. How you react when the apple machine eats your quarter or what you do when the ticket window you have waited hours to reach closes three persons in front of you—these make a difference. They are building experiences. It is the everyday prices and not the seasonal sales that determine a store's character and clientele. Similarly, the consistent careful choices, the daily decisions shape the nature of a man or woman.

Esther's great contribution to her people was made not as a climactic achievement of a long-pursued goal, but in her readiness to respond to a current crisis.

Esther's heroic stand in a time of great peril not only saved her people but has given others courage to encounter the problems of life. Her selfless allegiance to the people of the Lord inspires our dedication and loyalty. In this way her life's contribution was not for one time only, but a legacy to succeeding generations and peoples.

Great lives have enduring imprint. Joshua could say that he and his house would serve the Lord because in choosing for himself he established a way of life for his family and although he could not control their every action he provided a model that was their legacy.

In our more recent history, too, we find people who lived such lives that they became examples.

Sarah Melissa Granger was just fifteen years old when she went to Nauvoo to join the Saints. It was the Nauvoo of the early 1840s, with the persecution beginning and the Saints pushing to complete the temple, for they knew that when the temple was finished they could become a covenant people.

Sarah was very interested in the doctrine and revelations of her newfound church. She attended the School of the Prophets, and discussed the principles she learned there with her father. In later years she referred to her attendance at the School of the Prophets to underscore the importance she placed upon doctrinal study among Latter-day Saint women.

When she was about twenty-two, she married Hiram Kimball. Sarah was a member of the Church. Hiram Kimball was not. He was later baptized, but when their first baby was born the Nauvoo Temple walls were only about three feet above their foundation. The Saints needed money to complete the building. Sarah wanted to make a contribution to the temple project, but she wanted it to be her contribution, not her husband's. Even though he was well off financially and could afford to give generously to the Church, that didn't meet her needs as she saw them. She thought a great deal about how she could fulfill her responsibility. Then she came up with an idea. She had a new baby boy just three days old. When her husband came to her bedside to admire the baby, she asked,

"What is the boy worth?"

He replied, "Oh, I don't know, he's worth a great deal."

"Is he worth a thousand dollars?'

The reply was, "Yes, more than that if he lives and does well."

Sarah said, "Half of him is mine, is it not?"

"Yes, I suppose so."

"Then I have something to help on the temple," she said.

"You have?" her husband said pleasantly.

"Yes, and I am thinking of turning my share (of the baby) right in as tithing."

"Well, I'll see about that," said her husband.

Soon after that conversation her husband, who was a major in the Nauvoo Legion, met the Prophet Joseph Smith. Hiram said, "Sarah has got a little advantage of me this time, she proposes to turn over the boy as Church property."

President Joseph Smith seemed pleased with the joke and said, "I accept all such donations, and from this day the boy shall stand recorded, Church Property." He turned to Willard Richards and directed, "Make a record of this, and you are my witness."

"Major, you now have the privilege of paying $500 and retaining possession, or receiving $500 and giving possession." To which the new father responded, "How will that reserve block of property north of the Temple suit (as payment)?"

"It is just what we want," said the Prophet.

The deed was made out. Later the Prophet said to Sarah, "You have consecrated your first born son, for this you are blessed of the Lord . . . your name shall be handed down in honorable remembrance from generation to generation." (*Representative Women of Deseret*, compiled and written by Augusta Joyce Crocheron [J. C. Graham & Company, 1884], pp. 25-26.)

Sarah Kimball could translate her vision of the eternal truths into daily living. Perhaps her life was best described by a woman who knew her well, who said, "The name Sarah M. Kimball is synonymous with charity."

But what of you in your time? You find yourself in years of expectation and growth, unsure of the opportunities and difficulties that life in your future will provide for you. You are here to prepare, and prepare you must. You must develop the intellectual integrity and spiritual strength that will be a reservoir sufficient to meet each challenge with knowledge and testimony. Just as we store food against uncertain need, we must treasure up wisdom and truth that will enable us and future generations to meet each day's certain need with confidence, independent of the circumstances in which it is manifest.

A story told by Elder Vaughn J. Featherstone reminds us that "one life is all we have." He got it from Paul Harvey's *The Rest of the Story*, a Doubleday book published in 1977. It reminds us that the way we live life can influence others endlessly.

At the height of the gangster era in Chicago there was an attorney who was renowned for his ability to keep his mobster clients out of jail. Few have been as adept at manipulating legal procedures to protect their criminal clients. As his reputation grew so did his wealth and after a time he had acquired a large estate in the suburbs of Chicago and had married well.

Shortly after his marriage he and his wife had their first child, a son. As this young attorney reflected on the legacy that he would leave his son, he quickly saw that the wealth and reputation as an attorney for the underworld were worth little when compared to a legacy of honor, courage, and truth.

The attorney determined that, although it may cost him his life, he would go to the police and reveal the knowledge that he had of the criminal activities of the mob. When he approached the police they cautioned him, saying they could never provide sufficient protection to ensure his safety. Despite their caution he gave them information that led to the convictions of several leading members of the mob.

Less than a year after this testimony the young attorney was gunned down by associates of those he had helped convict. Still he had left his son the legacy of honor, truth, and courage that he had hoped to leave.

In another story of heroism, a young man called Butch O'Hare, while serving as an aviator in the Pacific during World War II, was forced on an occasion to return from his squadron to the aircraft carrier because of mechanical difficulties with his fighter plane.

While returning he spotted a squadron of Japanese zeros preparing to attack his carrier. Although far outnumbered and with a partially disabled plane, Butch O'Hare attacked the squadron of

Zeros and through his heroism saved the lives of many of his comrades as he demonstrated his courage and skill by disabling plane after plane from the Japanese squadron.

For his courage young Butch O'Hare received numerous citations and awards, including the honor of having the airport in his home town of Chicago named for him: "O'Hare International."

These two stories of courage are more than geographically related. The father of the World War II flying ace Butch O'Hare was the young attorney who had given his life so that he could leave his young son a legacy of courage and honor.

At eighty years of age my father had to have his leg amputated, which made the last year of his life particularly difficult. Speaking at his funeral, Elder Thomas S. Monson said:

> I suppose his greatest battle has occurred in the last few months, but he rose to the occasion and he demonstrated to each one of us that he is the man that we knew him to be. I've seen courage many times—in the Navy, in life. I've read about courage. But I don't know when I've seen courage to excell that of my friend as he overcame the handicap of a lost vital limb and to the amazement of the doctors, at his age, developed the ability to use his artificial limb in such a way that he could be proud of his accomplishment and could do many things that other people felt he never again would do.

These words and my father's example have been a rich legacy of continuing strength for me and our entire family, far more important than the earthly treasures of wealth or position he probably would have liked to have left us, but didn't.

The queen, a prophet in embryo, the athlete, the medical student, the wife, the soldier, the pilot, the attorney, the Relief Society leader, my father, all were surrounded by difficult circumstances not of their choosing, but the decisions they had earlier made prepared them to respond courageously.

It was so with Jesus. His day-by-day decisions prepared him to be the greatest example of courage known to mankind. Remember his question when his anxious mother found him in the temple? "How is it that ye sought me? wist ye not that I must be about my Father's business?" (Luke 2:49.) And yet, obedient to his parents, he went down with them to Nazareth and was subject to them. Because of that he increased in wisdom and stature and in favor with God and man. Jesus was tested and tried. He made choices knowing that man *should* live by every word that proceedeth out of the mouth of God, that he should not tempt the Lord but worship and serve him only. (See Matthew 4.)

His flawless character and the evidence of his pure love was revealed when he cried from the cross: "Father, forgive them; for they know not what they do" (Luke 23:34).

Each person must prepare to be of good courage by making good decisions daily and thus being ready to respond "greatly" in the testing moments of challenge that will surely come.

20

A Season for Strength

Good solutions often lie not so much in the undiscovered as in the unused.

When the Lord restored the gospel to the earth in its fulness and purity, he also organized the Church as a means to turn precepts into living principles, to help believers become Saints. And become Saints they did when, as converts, they were drawn by their compelling faith to put precept to the test, and in the strengths of the Lord they saw goals achieved, hopes realized, and their own strength grow.

In a gripping account of the Martin Handcart Company, caught by early winter storms in the trek from Iowa City to Salt Lake Valley, we read of "Margaret Dalglish, a stout Scottish girl worn down to skin and bones, but still keeping up." After wading through rivers of slushy ice, and suffering blizzards, hunger, and loss of loved ones, she was among those who were still "hauling their battered carts, still walking defiantly on their own legs" as they entered the valley at last.

While the demands made upon women in pioneer days may seem to be of more heroic proportions than those commonly faced by women today, in a sense, we share the whole range of problems—disease, divorce, drugs, death, immorality, economic insecurity, abuse, loneliness, depression, single parenthood— and on and on—problems with which women have always struggled and with which they now must contend.

We are in a time when the swift changes of our social structure are thrusting enormous challenges upon us. We must remember that the work of women is important and still must be done. The spirit children of God must have the experience of mortality, and that means babies must be wanted, nurtured, loved, and cared for. The Lord has given to women a primary responsibility in the establishment of good homes and well-cared-for families and, no matter what the challenges are, we must find ways to accomplish this life-giving and eternal work. Good family life is never an accident; it is always an achievement. It was so for the women of the past and it is so for us today. Our lives require discipline, coping without compromise, conversion of precepts into living principles that will make us saintly. We can see examples about us today.

Consider the sister, just recently baptized, who accepted a calling to teach a Relief Society lesson. When she could not arrange transportation one Sunday morning, she walked the eleven miles to the meetinghouse and gave her lesson in order to honor her commitment.

A visit by a Relief Society president to an inactive deaf sister revealed that it hurt the sister too much to go to meetings and never be able to join in the discussion. As the president left that home, she promised the sister if she would attend her Relief Society meetings she would be included. The president and her entire board learned to "sign." Gratitude, satisfaction, and personal enrichment came as this new skill was employed to respond to the need of that one individual.

The husband of a Relief Society sister was killed in a disastrous automobile accident, leaving his wife and three young children without means of support or much security. Upon taking stock of her circumstances, personal resources, and talents, the courageous wife worked out a plan whereby she could complete her education and provide financial sustenance for the family during the hours the children were in school. Through the application of thrift, discipline, and reliance on the Lord, the needs of the family were met. Kind, loving care was given to the sister's aged parents as well.

Even as the Lord organized the Church, we who have the gospel need also to organize our lives to do what has to be done, to become "doers of the word" (James 1:22), and in the doing come to know strength in the Lord. That strength comes when we prepare for his blessings, recognize them, and use his gifts to make his ways our ways.

In the beloved Latter-day Saint hymn "O My Father," Eliza R. Snow celebrates in words the continuity of family relationships beyond death and reminds us of a glorious reunion with our heavenly parents. Written as solace to a dear friend, Zina Huntington Young, who had lost her mother and father in tragic deaths, the well-known lines of this hymn give poetic statement to a great truth revealed through the Prophet Joseph Smith.

By looking closely, we can find in that single incident in Church history some of the gifts God has given to strengthen Latter-day Saint women: revealed truth, priesthood leadership, individual talents, and opportunities for service. These are available to every woman and can give us the power to triumph over the most difficult circumstance and move forward in strength.

In just rendering compassionate service to a friend, Eliza R. Snow used her talents, responded to priesthood leadership, and gave memorable expression to revealed truth.

In a very real sense, when Joseph Smith knelt in the Sacred Grove and asked his question, it was for each of us. The answer he received provides a sure foundation of fundamental truths upon which we should structure our lives. He also demonstrated that through personal prayer eternal truths answer individual needs. Heavenly power can help us understand and relate the timeless to our immediate concerns.

Whatever your circumstances, this can be your season of strength, because one of the most compelling concepts in the gospel is that the Savior will come again. And he counsels, "Behold, I come quickly" (Revelation 3:11). We must live with constant anticipation of his coming, being ready to receive him in the position of our greatest strength. Let this be our bulwark against temptation or slothfulness. Let it cause us to read the Savior's words, to search our hearts, and to try to live every principle of righteousness he taught. This will require us to love as he loves. Then, we are told, when he comes we shall know him, for we shall be like him (see 1 John 3:2).

21
The Woman's Part

Whatever else we have learned from the parable of the prodigal son, this, too, we ought to remember—after the younger son had wasted his inheritance and was in the extremity of need, he looked to his home for help. And when he returned there, fortune-spent and world-weary, his home was prepared to assist. Along with a model of Christlike forgiveness and unconditional love, we see in this story an emphasis on the need for every family to provide for each of its members. Although the nature and source of the need may differ from that of the prodigal son, the welfare of each member of the family is the responsibility of the family.

Women will play a vital role in bringing about support, not "in the place of" or "as substitute for something else," but as a role in itself, necessary to successful undertakings.

The little boy who wanted his mother to come play with him understood the importance but not the full nature of support. He pleaded with her until she finally left her work to come play darts with him. Excitedly, he explained his game plan, saying, "Now I'll throw the darts and you stand there and say, 'Wonderful, wonderful!' "

While his need may have been childish, the little boy unerringly touched upon a principle that promotes achievement. When encouraged, individuals can accomplish much. Women give encouragement, but they do much, much more than that. They promote mastery of some fundamental principles that provide the base for charitable living. For example, wives and mothers can instill an attitude of frugality and thrift that makes it possible for each family member to have a part in contributing to those in need. Women who demonstrate sacrifice and faithfulness will encourage greater response to calls for assistance. Every woman, too, can learn through the life of Jesus the Christ to assume her advocacy role as she represents the cause of the needy and suffering, as she is advocate for her children with the world, and as she advocates the work of the Lord for the good of all of his children.

The ability to give encouragement works in many places.

One of the most effective ways that Relief Society can support and give encouragement to the priesthood leadership of the Church, for instance, is through the council system. Women can bring to each council a special sensitivity and insight to family and individual needs. Through organized assignments, women encourage them as well.

When two visiting teachers went to the home of an elderly sister and her husband, both of whom were recovering from serious illness, they noted more than once, when they asked the ailing sister how she was getting along, she replied, "We're better, but our house is so dirty." Their home was not disorderly, but it exuded a faint dinginess that suggested months without a thorough cleaning. The visiting teachers understood the discouragement that this condition was beginning to foster.

The Relief Society president reported the plight of the elderly couple in the next welfare committee meeting. Other committee members, recognizing this as a welfare need, suggested ways they, too, might help. And on an appointed day, not only were walls, windows, and floors cleaned, but cupboards were scrubbed and curtains laundered, lawns were thatched and a garden plot made ready for planting. How much better prepared, then, were these two to do what they could to meet their own welfare needs.

The compassionate nature of a woman's perspective to bring forth the potential power of her family in the support of worthy projects is vital.

The success of family preparedness is begun in the home. As a man and a woman working together prayerfully plan for the welfare of their family, they take the first step toward a provident home. A single woman living alone or with her family can be equally successful in providing individual preparedness. A family organization is, in a remarkable sense, a reflection of the Church. Church participation, then, is a kind of family preparedness. Individual spiritual growth and family strength result when Church leadership is a pattern for family leadership.

Our family, recognizing a potential for growth, organized and held a family meeting. A committee was appointed for overall planning of events including an opening session, separate meetings for the men and the women, and a closing session, followed by a dinner. My husband presided over the meeting, assignments were made well in advance for talks, musical numbers, printing of programs, and for recording the proceedings that were to become part of our family's history.

A home might also serve as an effective visitors' center where gospel precepts are displayed in an obvious but not pretentious way and are freely shared with guests.

We could also teach of a storehouse in each home, where the abundance of a garden is providently processed and where children are assigned responsibilities that promote self-reliance.

It would be equally possible to create in every home a missionary training center. A mother might give as homemaking instruction to her potential missionary sons and daughters some things she has learned in Relief Society homemaking miniclasses. Or think of the preparation a woman can foster when she, through Relief Society lessons and personal study, becomes so imbued with the Spirit of the Lord that she can teach her children the truths of the gospel.

Studying together, they will learn those answers which the Savior knew and taught and which he used when faced with temptation. Jesus demonstrates in Luke 4 how knowledge of the scriptures can confound the blandishments of Satan. To each temptation the Savior replied, "It is written . . . ," teaching us of the necessity for knowledge if we would have power over evil.

Mothers who realize that children must be taught the ways of the Lord if they are to counter the ways of the world, and that no one can teach children righteous behavior better than parents, will recognize the importance of their role in protecting and preserving their families. A woman can make her home a place of extraordinary opportunity as she learns the full meaning of preparedness—of food and clothing, of knowledge and spiritual strength, of love and compassion. She can make home a place from which every family member will go forth, not prodigal-like, but with the inheritance of the full armor of the Lord.

I was flying to Arkansas recently. Outside it was raining and the woman sitting in the seat next to me said: "I love to be at home when it rains. I like to hurry and make something that smells good as it bakes, build a fire in the fireplace, prepare a kettle of soup to keep warm on the stove. Then I put on my favorite music and get out my ironing board and work there in front of the fire until everyone comes home. I love to see them come in and warm themselves by the fire and then have a bowl of soup and some fresh bread hot from the oven."

When the storms of life cause us to turn toward home, we yearn for a refuge and the security that home alone can give. There can be the power of continual revelation of the Lord, his strength to care for the poor among us and see that every home becomes a bulwark against the vicissitudes of the world.

A woman's part in the world today has many definitions. There really is no single statement to cover her work or her assignments. Being an eternal soul, she defies an easy categorization. Any rigid stereotype breaks down upon examination.

A woman's part has to do with giving life and solving problems and responding to human need. The woman's part is to fill herself with ideas, with learning, with excellence in the mastery of skills, and with love, the love that never faileth. The woman's part is to give generously to help solve the great challenges that arise at home and in the community. The woman's part is to fill her home with love as a great reservoir from which all may come and receive renewal. The woman's part is to be the faithful disciple who follows the Master, the Lord Jesus Christ.

Epilogue

On Accepting an
Honorable Release

This afternoon I feel somewhat like a former chief justice of Ontario, Canada, who explained his feelings on his ninety-fifth birthday anniversary. In his mind Sir William Mulock rationalized, "it's just another birthday like all the others." But as he stood to acknowledge the occasion his words revealed a love of life, a love of his work and of his fellowmen. He said:

> "I have warmed both hands before the fire of life. . . . The rich spoils of memory are mine. . . . Mine, too, are the precious things of today. . . . The best of life is always further on. Its real lure is hidden from our eyes somewhere behind the hills of time." (Lillian Eichler Watson, ed., *Light from Many Lamps* [Simon & Schuster, 1951], pp. 267-68.)

Like that grand old man, I love life. I love the work in which I have been engaged for the past nine and a half years—the demanding, intense, but beautiful work of Relief Society. It has been so sweet to me that it has seemed but a fleeting moment in time.

Talk given in general conference on April 7, 1984, after having been released as general president of the Relief Society.

As I stand at this point of transition, a montage of memories crowd my mind: of family, my good husband supporting and patiently waiting for me, of my children and their mates struggling to arrange their busy schedules to meet mine, and of grandchildren often being my examples; of the women with whom I have worked—a kaleidoscope of images, experiences, and impressions comes to me of them.

I see my devoted, talented, loyal counselors, Marian R. Boyer, Janath R. Cannon, Shirley W. Thomas, and Ann S. Reese, and my secretary-treasurer, Mayola R. Miltenberger, all of whom I dearly love; I see the brilliant, gifted women who have served with me on the Relief Society General Board. And there is my personal secretary and the dear women of our staff, the hostesses who serve in the Relief Society building, our public communications representative, Moana B. Bennett.

I also see the faithful stake and ward Relief Society leaders and the many, many sisters who constitute the membership of Relief Society throughout the Church whom I have come to know and appreciate.

At this moment, I can only echo President Kimball's words: "God bless the women!—the *wonderful, wonderful* women!" (*Relief Society Magazine,* January 1958, p. 8.)

Certainly I have "warmed both my hands at the fires of their lives . . ."

I have seen nobility emerge as I have observed them overcome personal sorrows, disappointments, and tragedies. I have witnessed their compassion and loving ministrations, both within their families and toward their neighbors. I have savored their creativity, rejoiced in their achievements, and shared their joyous moments.

I have felt the strength of our sisterhood as we have met in Sunday Relief Society meetings, in women's area conference meetings, in socials, and in significant historical events such as the memorable occasion in Nauvoo, the birthplace of our beloved organization, where we memorialized that event with a beautiful garden of monuments to women.

I've read how Relief Society observed its fiftieth year with a great gathering of sisters in the Tabernacle. President Zina D. H. Young addressed the congregation and exclaimed:

> O that my words could be heard by all people, not only by you my brethren and sisters in this tabernacle but that they might be *heard* and *understood* by all the people of this continent, and not only this continent, but the continents of Asia, Africa, Europe and the islands of the sea. (Minutes of the Relief Society General Board, Vol. 1, March 17, 1892, p. 225.)

I have come to feel this may have been more than just a wistful expression of a great former leader. Perhaps it was instead a pleading with the Lord for a time such as this. Let me explain: When I was a little girl I participated in a program here in the Tabernacle. At that time an impression came to me that I have never forgotten, even though I did not understand it then. I was filled with an awareness that sometime I would stand before a vast congregation of the Church in this building.

I thought this vision of my childhood was realized in the 1974 Relief Society conference when I was sustained as the general president of the Relief Society. But now I feel certain that *this* is the day I saw. And perhaps because of prayerful people like President Zina Young our voices are heard proclaiming the truths of the gospel to all the world—truths that can be transmitted into the very hearts and minds of people who will listen and try to understand.

In that spirit I am proud to testify today that our prophets and apostles are men called of God. They will always lead the Church aright by divine direction and by the power of the holy priesthood of God.

The women of the Church have an important work to do. That work requires great strength of character, faith in the Lord Jesus Christ, and a pure heart that will be a light unto the world and a bulwark of righteousness against the darkness that covers the earth with contention and evil.

In all humility I declare my ever-expanding love for you. I assure you, too, that I deeply love our newly called and sustained general president of the Relief Society. I know the Relief Society is in good hands. It will continue to grow and move forward in countless ways to bless the lives of all of the daughters of God.

I know this is true. I feel it with every fiber of my being, just as I know that God lives, that Jesus is the Christ, our Savior and our Redeemer.

May we all make the most of every moment of our lives, that "somewhere beyond the hills of time" we will be with them again.

Index